15.95

F

THE
Broonie,
Silkies
& Fairies

ALSO BY
DUNCAN WILLIAMSON

*Fireside Tales of the
Traveller Children*

THE
Broonie, Silkies & Fairies

Travellers' Tales of the Other World

BY
Duncan Williamson
ILLUSTRATED BY
Alan B. Herriot

HARMONY BOOKS
NEW YORK

Published in the United States in 1987 by Harmony Books, a division of Crown Publishers, Inc., 225 Park Avenue South, New York, New York 10003 and represented in Canada by the Canadian MANDA Group.
Originally published in Scotland by Canongate Publishing Limited, 17 Jeffrey Street, Edinburgh, Scotland.
HARMONY and colophon are trademarks of Crown Publishers, Inc.
Manufactured in the United States of America

Library of Congress Cataloging-in-Publication Data
Williamson, Duncan.
The broonie, silkies, and fairies.

Contents: The silkie's revenge—The broonie on
Carra—Saltie the silkie—[etc.]
1. Tales—Scotland. 2. Folklore—Scotland.
[1. Folklore—Scotland] I. Herriot, Alan, ill.
II. Title.
GR144.W533 1985   398.2′09411   86-29415
ISBN 0-517-56525-0

10 9 8 7 6 5 4 3 2 1
First American Edition

to Kim,
who never knew what a silkie was

CONTENTS

EDITOR'S NOTE

Duncan Williamson began telling stories to public audiences in 1976, when, in view of the non-traveller society's interest, he realized his responsibility as a tradition bearer.

All my stories I've told you these past years belong to dead people—they're all gone. And that's why I want to tell them to you and to the world, because some day I'm not going to be around and I want people to remember and enjoy the stories that were passed down from generations of people, from the West Coast to Aberdeenshire, through Angus to Perthshire, down into Ayrshire, around the Borders, and all over—these beautiful stories that were not written down but were traditional.

The nature of telling traditional stories as a performing rather than a creative art is shown by Duncan's conservative attitude towards his tradition.

You may think it strange that I don't make up any stories. I couldn't, suppose you paid me for it. I can make up a song of the present day but it's just not within me to make up a story. I wouldn't believe it! All these stories I'm telling you I have collected and found along my travels. They meant so much to me because I was really interested. I was reared, born and bred on stories; that's all I had in my life.

This collection of Duncan's West Highland tales* stems mostly from his early years in Argyll, 1935–43. His narrations of silkie, broonie, and fairy stories were recorded on tapes now lodged in the archives of the School of Scottish Studies after the resounding success of his first book, *Fireside Tales of the Traveller Children.* My catalogue of Duncan's three hundred and fifty narrations, a fraction of his repertoire, includes at least thirty silkie, broonie, and fairy stories not yet published. The twelve finally chosen for the book have an "Other World" theme, with a moral thrust which belies a common perception of travellers throughout Scotland.

All these stories are a matter of teaching, to show what can happen to you if you are evil and bad or good and kind. Because the travellers have met with so much badness, so much opposition and persecution along the way in their lives, even the thought of badness in their minds disturbs them. They believe that nobody in the world has any reason to be bad. They never hurt anybody. They live their own lives, do their own things and want to be left alone—like the seals.

I should like to acknowledge the assistance of the Scottish Arts Council and lecturers in the School of Scottish Studies, particularly David Clement and Margaret Bennett, who gave me most helpful advice on editing the transcriptions of my husband's tales for this publication. I am grateful to Archibald

---

*Most of the stories take place on the West Coast, which Duncan defines as an area extending from Kintyre north to Appin and inland from Campbeltown to Glen Fyne.

Kenneth for his useful comments on the native speakers of Loch Fyne, and to Hamish Henderson for his excellent coaching on the final draft of the manuscript.

Linda Williamson
Kincraigie, Strathmiglo, 1985

INTRODUCTION

Silkies and the Other World

The word "silkie" is derived from the softness of the skin of a seal. My granny had a piece of seal-skin and it could forecast the weather: before a storm the hair rises up, telling you it's going to be rough; when the sun comes out the seal-skin lies smooth and soft and silky.

Travellers believe seals are just folk, sea-people. "Silkies" means the same to them as "seal-folk" or "seal-people." Not all seals are silkies, but some can take over the form of a human being, be a human, or take away a human to become a seal. This was taught down through the ages among the travelling folk.

Where do the stories come from? I really got more silkie stories from the country folk than from the travellers. Most of the stories started with those non-travellers who had wee crofts on the shore. A croft was a house and wee bit of ground, maybe the land was not much bigger than a large garden. Crofting folk grew a few vegetables, kept a few goats, maybe a couple of pet lambs or some hens, and some days they spent in their boats on the sea. They had a wee net and they caught fish, kippered and salted them, and what they couldn't use they probably took along and sold in the wee villages. That was all the source of work that some had. How was a man with a wee croft going to keep three, maybe four, sons in work unless they went to the fishing? The sea was plentiful and there was a good demand. Some took up lobsters and some fished for crabs, some even gathered whelks.

So when the crofting folk told stories among themselves and to their weans, it was probably seal stories and silkie stories. Storytelling was their main source of entertainment. And these folk would never have made these stories up, or else they'd never have believed them!

How the seal stories of the West Coast were passed down to the travelling folk is not hard to understand. The travellers camped along the shores of the Western Isles. They drank in pubs with the non-traveller men. And it was natural for the lonely old fisherman or crofter coming along the shoreside at night from a bar-room, who saw a tinkers' fire, to come into the campsite with a bottle of whisky in his pocket. He sat down by their fireside and gave the old men a drink, and he probably told a story! And once he started telling the travellers about the seals, they became so interested that any animosity towards this man (for being a non-traveller) went out of their minds till the story was finished. They drank whisky with him, bade him "good-night," and he went on his way.

The travellers were very attached to seals. In the past, privileged camping for many was on the shoresides, which were good to nobody else. A large part of many travellers' lives was spent camped right on the beaches. Here they were out of the way. All that was seen to people passing by on the road was smoke coming from their fires. And travellers enjoyed the seals, their company. When they played their pipes and sang their songs, made music round the campfires, the seals used to gather out and listen. I've seen them dozens of times! My father used to take the bagpipes, walk along the shore, and play tunes to the seals. And the thing was—they loved it! Their heads would pop out of the water and they'd sit up straight. It was the greatest thing in the world to see fifteen to twenty seals gathered, all listening, looking in different directions, and him playing the pipes to them. Seals are very fond of music, any kind. Even if you whistle they will come right up to you. That's what attracted travelling folk to seals in the first place.

My father was a great believer in the seal-folk. He believed the seals would even come at night and throw stones at you if you were bad to them during the day. I remember him telling me the seals or the silkies will never do you any harm, not unless you are bad to them. Then they set out to teach you a lesson. If you are good to them, then all good things happen, you get what you want. Silkies are only out to protect their own families, the same as the travellers. And travellers have no fear of being taken away with the silkies: they think by going with the silkie and joining in the seal-folk's world they will have a better way of life. And they look forward to it.

So when there comes a story about the seal-folk, the travellers really love it. To them it is something of the world they would love to be in, if they could have the power . . . and they believe some day they will. Power only comes to you by believing in something, and they believe these stories. You might live a hundred years and never come in contact with a silkie, but that doesn't mean such a thing doesn't exist. You believe me, the world of the silkie exists till this day!

The Fairies

Now there are many wonderful things you can learn about fairies, and things connected with fairy stories. Why should fairies be connected with the first of May? Well, according to legend and the travelling folk's idea about the Other World, all the different beings have their own places: witches, for instance, are connected to old houses in forests, kelpies are in waterfalls, the broonie in old mills and old buildings, and fairies have their fairy hills. And the travellers say, in their cracks and tales and stories, that the fairies are shut up under the hills all winter, for nine months of the year. When it comes to the first of May, the King of the Fairies lets them loose, sets them free for three months to do as they please And they do plenty, you believe me! Nobody hardly ever sees

any fairies, but the proof is there. They work among flowers
and work among plants, helping Mother Nature. And at the
end of July the fairies are gone. But they are so excited when
they are set free at the beginning of summer, they have their
party, their ceilidh; and lucky is the person who is in this
very place on the first of May!

Travellers never bother so much about the fairies in the
wintertime, when the fairies are away in their own place. But
I know folk who won't camp in certain places in the summer
where they might camp in the winter, because travellers don't
want to annoy the fairies: "Oh, that's a fairy place . . . !"
They have their beliefs in the fairies all right.

The travelling folk will do nothing that would insult the
fairies. Taking wee moths and pulling their wings off, or
killing a butterfly in the summertime, or pulling the heads off
the wee flowers—that's evil, according to the tradition, that
would bother the fairies. You see, travellers travel a lot during
the summer months with their weans. Now, they don't like
them to be cruel—no way in this world—and hurt wee animals and pull wee flowers. You know the contrivances of
weans, they'll get into wicked things. And they are taught
that to do these things will upset the fairies. It is a kind of
code, a discipline to keep them in hand. For example, you
don't touch a moth—it could be a fairy in disguise. Moths and
butterflies are associated with the fairies. You see, if the old
travellers had got a curse put on them, they made a butterfly
out of the tree bark, sure! That was to break the curse. They
cut a strip of bark and made a shape of a butterfly and kept it
till the curse went off them.

Aye, there are many cracks and tales about the fairies with
the travellers, they're deep in belief with the fairies. There's
plenty of folk believe they have heard "a fairy tune," music
played on the fairy pipes or the fairy fiddle. And if anybody is
a good piper, the travellers say he can "play like a fairy,"
meaning he plays the right notes in the right manner.

The fairies never teach people lessons, but they have "gifted" people. If a traveller woman is really good at reading hands, telling fortunes truthfully, travellers say that woman has "the gift fae the wee folk." The gift was not made to her, but to her mother and her mother before her and her mother before her—you see, the gift passes on. And if a wean is clever—can stand at six months or walk at nine months—they say, "Oh, that wean's gifted . . ."

In the summertime if a wean is born to a fairy at the same time as a wee wean is born to a mortal, and the fairies know their baby is going to grow up to be a "mongol" and is never going to be right, they won't keep it. The fairies only keep babies that are going to be healthy, strong, and clever. So, before they would destroy or kill a deficient baby, they will switch it over: they will go and take a mortal wean and put in its place their one, and let the mortal folk look after it. In the story of the "Taen-Awa," the fairy wean that comes is evil. It knows it isn't in its own dominion and that its own folk have put it away among strangers. That's why it cries so much—to return the fairies' wicked deed. But the travellers have a protection against the fairies, you see! My mother used to stick a needle in the wean's bonnet at night-time—the fairies can't take the wean as long as something made of steel is fastened to its clothes. Oh, the fairies steal babies during the three months of summer! And some travellers never get their weans back. Some are wee delinquent weans all the days of their lives. If there is a retarded person in the family, travellers believe this wean was given to them when their own one was "taen awa." But they love it just the same; even though it is bad and wicked, it is still loved.

The Broonie and God

The country folk's beliefs in the Broonie are just as strong as any traveller's, in fact maybe a wee bit stronger. Old Duncan McVicar, the Gaelic-speaking farmer I used to work for at

Auchinagoul, he wouldn't mention his name at all—just called him "the wee fella." It was the same as the travellers' belief in God; they won't say his name either—it's the "Good Man" they call him, the same name for Jesus.

The Broonie can take any form if he wants to. But he doesn't come to deceive people, rather to test them, so he comes in the form of the lonely old tramp with a ragged coat, the lowest form of life, who is thought of as nothing. It's like God coming in another form. As a tramp he will get the person's true personality, the person's true feelings towards the lowest type of person you could ask for! He always says he is hungry because giving is better than receiving! The people who would give and feed the Broonie would give and feed somebody else. The people who would turn away the Broonie as a tramp are not good people at all.

Broonie stories are different from other kinds of story: they have no happy ending, they only have a lesson. That's why the Broonie couldn't come as a king or a prince, not as a soldier or policeman or priest. If the Broonie came in the form of a minister, how was he going to walk up to a house and teach people a lesson? If a priest or a doctor or a lawyer came to a body's house, they would change completely; they wouldn't be theirsel but putting on a front to welcome a high person.

No, the Broonie always comes in the same form—the wee old tramp man, about five feet tall, with the wee white beard and the two blue eyes, the kindly old creature of a man who never insults, never hurts, is always looking for work and he's always hungry. His famous meal, he loves a bowl of porridge and milk, or a bowl of soup. It's something that goes back many many years, long before your time and mine, long before Christianity . . . about the supernatural being who was cast down to take care of us, the humble folk.

You see, the Broonie is a spirit that never dies. It isn't exactly the blueness of his eyes, it's their brightness and youth! The travellers believe dullness is a sign of old age; so, as far as they believe, the brightness of the blue eyes is to show that youth and the spirit *are in his eyes*.

The Broonie, the silkies, and the fairies are the same to the travellers, for they have their strong beliefs in them all: they're part of an Other World for travellers that they love. Because the people of this Other World have the freedom, have the power, they are immune from persecution by the local public and can't be disturbed. People of the Other World are part of nature—same as the travelling folk.

The
Silkie's
Revenge

ow many years ago in a wee village on the West Coast there lived a minister. He hadn't a very big parish. Houses in these days were kind o' thinly scattered. He didn't have a big congregation coming to his church, so he had a lot of time to spend to himself. Mostly all ministers in these days kept a boat for to do a bit o' fishing in their spare time. And having his manse by the shoreside, he had a boat and did a bit o' fishing, but he also had a net that he set sometimes for fish. And he used to give a lot of fish away to the people of the village who weren't able to fish for themselves. He was quite happily married with his wife and one wee girl. But he had a terrible anger against the seals—because these nets were very hard to get and it cost a lot of money to buy one—every morning when he went down he found holes in his net, some of his fish were eaten and destroyed. Even though he was the minister, he swore revenge on the seals.

On Sunday mornings before he went to church, he always used to go down and lift his net early before the tide went out so the gulls wouldn't go near his fish. He went down to the net one Sunday morning early and there caught was a wee baby seal—it wasn't very old, maybe a week and no more. It was still alive! And the funny thing—not a fish was touched in his net, there was a lot of fish in the net.

But he took the wee baby seal by the flipper. "You little rascal!" he said. "You'll grow up some day to be a big seal and then you'll destroy my net if I'm still here." And he took

3

the wee baby seal, hit its head against a rock, and threw it among the seaweed on the shore. He turned round to take pieces of seaweed out of his net, and he looked out. About ten or fourteen feet out in the sea was a seal and its head was up out of the water—it was watching him. He shook his fist at it. And it disappeared in the water.

So he walked home with his fish to his wife and told her about his net and all his hate for the seals.

His wife, she was a *gentle kind o' cratur*.[1] "You know," she told him, "you should try and leave the seals alone. They're entitled to have as much fish oot o' the sea as what you have."

He said, "You can say what you like but I hate these creatures, you'll never get me to like them in any way."

So a few months later, the end of summer, his wife became very sick and they sent for the doctor. The doctor tried everything in the world to save her, but she just pined away and died. And the minister was very very upset. That period of time he never set a net or did any fishing; all his time was spent looking after his wee lassie Morag, who was only four years old.

But between doing his service in the church, doing his garden and his housework, he didn't have enough time left for the wee lassie, his boat, and his net. He advertised in a local newspaper for a housekeeper, which usually they did in these days when there was too much to do.

About a week passed and one day he and his little girl were sitting at their wee bit o' supper when a knock came to the door.

And the wee lassie said, "Daddy, I'll go and see who it is."

He thought it was some o' the folk from the village or something. The wee girl went to the door and there stood this woman in her mid-thirties. Her father shouted to her, "Who is it, Morag?"

---

[1]*gentle kind o' cratur*—kindly soul

She said, "It's a lady, Daddy."

So the minister came walking out to the door and he said to this young woman, "Hello, what can I do for you?"

She said, "I saw your advertisement in the local newspaper, you're looking for a housekeeper."

"Yes," he said, "I am."

"Well," she said, "I've come about the job."

"Well," he said, "don't stand there at the door, come in!" So he took her into the house, asked her her name, where she came from.

She said she was a widow and her name was Selina.

"Look, you can stay in the house," he said, and he told her how much he was going to pay her. "The main purpose I want you for is to take care o' my little daughter because I havena much time, with my garden and my fishin, and," he said, "the child's mother has passed away."

"I'll take good care of her," she said.

So they agreed on a wage for her and he showed her where to stay, her bedroom, and she said that was all right.

"Now," he said, "ye can have your meals in the kitchen with me whenever you need to."

So he took a good look at her: she had long dark hair and brown eyes, a good-looking young woman she was, very quiet. But the moment the wee lassie saw her, wee Morag just took to her right away. She was a weak kind o' wee lassie, Morag, and the minister was quite happy.

So she was there for about two weeks and everywhere she went, Morag went with her. It was just like a second mother to her. The minister never paid attention for the first two or three weeks; he just thought it was the affection of the wee lassie after losing her mother—why she was clinging to this woman. And this Selina just loved this wee lassie, took her everywhere. During the evening when the minister was in his room doing his work for the church, writing his papers, learning his sermon and that, Selina would take wee Morag away with her along the beach and the minister thought nothing of it. And they would be gone for hours. And when she came back Morag seemed a happier and more radiant child than ever she was in her life. The minister was very pleased.

So she was there for about two months . . . whenever the wee girl came into the house and her daddy wanted to speak to her, it was just "Selina this" and "Selina that." She just sat in Selina's lap and cuddled her and the minister thought it kind of queer that she should think so much of her, you see. So even at mealtime, when they sat down to have their meal together, the two of them would just pick at their food, they wouldn't hardly eat anything. And this upset the minister too.

So as time went by he began to get really upset and he turned round and said to her, "Look, can we not have a decent meal together sometime?" And they were always so quiet, they couldn't wait till the meal was over till they got away on the beach. "Where do youse go every evening?" he said, "why do youse go, how do youse spend so much time on the beach—cold or wind or any day, you always go on the beach—can you not find comfort in here, in the manse with a good fire?"

"Morag loves to swim and," she said, "I always like to take her to the beach, we enjoy the beach together so much."

But another month passed by and the minister began to see that the lassie was slowly going away from him, clinging to this woman. So he made his mind up that he was going to either tell her off or give her the sack, or he was going to have a settlement with her. He made up his mind the next morning . . . he's going to take them fishing.

Now you know these wee rowing boats, there's a seat in the middle, a seat up in the front, and a seat across the back. The minister took his fishing rod and he said to Selina and Morag, "I want youse today to come fishin with me." So they went out fishing. And the minister's sitting rowing in the front of the boat with his rod in the bow, when he comes out just about where he'd seen the seal when he'd lifted his net that one Sunday morning—it wasn't far out from the beach. And Selina was sitting at the back of the boat, her arm round wee Morag's neck, and Morag and her were whispering to each other. This upset the minister so much.

"Look," he said to Selina, "what are ye tryin tae do to me; are you trying tae take my little girl from me, only thing I have left in this world now my wife is gone? I've been good to ye and I treated ye right in this place and I've let you do what you like. But now it's getting unbearable. I need Morag as much as you need her—in fact I prob'ly need her more. After all," he said, "she's my daughter, not yours! You're just tryin to take the only thing from me that I really love in this world."

And Selina turned round. "And you done the same for me!"

"Woman," he said, "I did nothing for you."

She said, "Look, you took the only thing that *I* really loved in this world, ye took my baby and hit its head against a stone!"

And the minister just stood aghast—he didn't know what to say, when Selina put her arm round Morag's neck and both of them went over the back of the boat and disappeared in the water. The bubbles came up and they were gone. From that day on, till the day he died, the minister never saw his daughter or Selina again.

————

This story was told to me by Neil McCallum, a stone-dyke mason of a crofting family, many years ago. His forbears had come from some of the islands in the Hebrides and this was one of his favorites. There are many stories about silkies that take in every type of person—farmers, shepherds, policemen— and, like this one, a minister.

The travellers had a good reason to believe in the silkies when they had stories like this! It's supposed to have been true . . . well, if it could happen to a minister it could happen to them, couldn't it?

The Broonie on Carra

own near Campbeltown in Argyll there's a wee island called Carra,[1] and the local villagers believe that that is the home of the Broonie, he stays on Carra. The island is small and there's only one house on it. There's water on Carra—I once walked down the steps cut out of stone to the Broonie's well, where he's supposed to drink his wee drop o' water. But otherwise Carra is uninhabited.

Now many years ago this minister, who was a great believer in the Broonie, bought the wee house on Carra and he and his wife moved out to the island. They lived very happily on Carra, they took a cow across with them to supply them with milk. The minister loved the island, he set lobster pots and he fished, did everything—he was quite happy and content. He had no family, just him and his wife.

So this minister had a boat and he used to travel across to Bellochantuy when he needed to go to Campbeltown for his messages. But in these days there were no cars on the road, it was only a track to Campbeltown, just a horsetrack, it was all done by pony and trap. Once a week he had to go across to the mainland to give a service in Campbeltown. He drove by pony and trap and always took his wife with him when he went. They would row their boat across from Carra, tie it up, borrow a pony and trap from a local farmer and drive to Campbeltown, do his service in the church and drive back,

[1]"Carrie" is what the local folk say

11

leave the pony and trap at the farm, and row across to Carra
to his house.

But one moring, it was a beautiful Sunday morning, his
cow was about to calf. So he said to his wife, "I think we'll
take the cow out." Now next to his house was a wee shed
where he kept a wee byre for holding the cow. He took the
cow out and said, "Poor sowl, you're better walkin aboot—
it'll help ye when ye're gaunnae have a calf, ye can walk
aboot, for you seem very sick." He let the cow go.

He and his wife went down, took the boat, rowed it across,
tied the boat up, borrowed the pony and trap from the farmer,
and drove to Campbeltown, which is about fifteen miles. (It's
not far for a horse, a horse'll do it in an hour and a half.) He
did his service in the church, came out of the church, talked to
his friends, yoked the horse, and left Campbeltown. But there
came a storm, a terrible time of rain and wind.

He said to his wife, "Come storm or hail or rain, we'll
have to get home tonight tae Carrie." But the weather got
worse.

He drove back the fifteen miles to Bellochantuy, then on to
Muasdale. When he came to Muasdale the weather was still
worse, you could hardly see—the rain was battering, the
waves were lashing!

And his wife turned round to him, "Husband, we'll never
get home tonight to Carrie, there's no way in the world that
we're gaunnae get across, take our own boat across tae Carrie
tonight!"

He says, "Wife, we'll hev tae! What about wir cow! What's
about the wee cow! It's out there itself, wanderin on the
island the night among this rain and sleet!"

They drove the horse back to the farm, drove up to the
house. The old farmer came out and met them. After the
horse had been tied up and its harness taken off, the minister
came in and had a cup of tea or a dram.

The waves were lashing and the boom was coming across
from Carra. So the old farmer said to the minister, "Look,

there's no way in the world you're gaunnae cross that sea tonight! For the peril o your wife's life . . ."

But the minister says, "What about my wee cow!"

He said, "Does the cow mean more to ye than your wife, or your own life?"

The minister said, "Look, the cow's wanderin the night—I let her loose before I left."

The farmer finally persuaded the minister that there's no way in the world he was going to take a boat across that night to Carra. It was impossible! Now the cow was on its own. The island is desolate, it's not very big, only about three acres, practically all rock. Not a soul is on the island, just the house, the byre, and the cow—no dogs, no cats, nothing.

The minister was very unhappy but he stayed in the farm, the old farmer put him and his wife up for the night. He passed a terrible sleepless night because he was thinking on his wee cow, in the island on its own, wandering alone with the cold and the wind, and it was going to calf.

But anyway, morning came, which it always does. And the minister was up bright and early, it was a beautiful day. The sea was calm, the wind was gone, the rain was gone, and there was hardly a wave to be seen. And he called his wife, he couldn't hurry quickly enough. They had a wee bit breakfast from the farmer and bade him good-bye, left the pony and trap for the farmer to take care of (the minister probably owned the trap), and hurried down across the road, about four hundred yards from the farm, through a wee field down to the boat.

The minister got in the boat and his wife got in the back. They were just a young couple, in their thirties, no children. He got into the oars and pulled the boat across as fast as he could. And och, the sea was as calm as the palm of your hand—not a wave, nothing. The sun was shining. He rowed across to Carra. And right where you land the boat is a wee place in the rocks, there's a few steps which go down to the Broonie's well—and water comes out of this rock face. The

minister pulls in the boat, and there's a bolt in the wall and a
ring to tie up your boat. He tied the boat to the ring, couldn't
hurry fast enough, helped his wife out of the boat, and the
two of them hurried up the wee shingle path to the house.

But before the minister went near the house he searched all
around as far as he could see, looking for the cow. Cow was
gone. He said to his wife, "She's prob'ly been blown over the
rocks and carried away in the tide."

Into the house the minister went. The wife made a cup of
tea and he was sitting down in his chair, completely sad and
broken-hearted because he loved this wee cow dearly. . . . It
was the only thing gave them milk on the wee island. They
loved the solitude and peace and quietness of this island, that's
why they went there in the first place, because he could think
about God and his sermons—he was a good man, a really
good man.

He said to his wife, "I'm really sorry . . . look what happened. Well, I'll take a wee walk and walk aroond the shoreside,
see if I can find the carcass o' her, she was prob'ly carried
away wi the tide."

But as he went outside he thought he'd have a last look
in the byre where he used to tie the wee cow up at night-
time. He said, "If I only had left her tied in the byre,
she'd be safe." Now he used to always fill a pail of water
for the cow and carry it in. And before he had gone away,
when he'd left the cow out on the grass, he'd carried the
pail and left it outside—he remembered this—that he'd
left the pail of water outside because there was no running water inside the wee byre. When he walked out the
door of the house, he looked at the door of the byre—
the pail was gone! He said, "I remember . . . I took the
pail oot and left the pail at the door when I let the coo
oot."

There was nothing to do—he walked to the byre, opened
the door, and walked into the byre. There was the wee cow
standing, a pail of water at her head, a beautiful heap of hay

in the wee *heck*[2] at her nose and the bonniest wee calf you ever saw standing at her feet! And the chain was round her neck, she was tied up, tied up to the stall where he had tied her before. The minister stood and he looked, he was aghast. He ran into the house, called his wife and told her to come out.

"Come oot," he said, "I want to show you something!"

"What is it?" she said.

"Come here, come here. I want to show you something! Look!" he said to his wife. He opened the door of the byre and he showed her—there was the cow and there was the bonnie wee calf standing at her feet, there was the pail of water and there was the hay in her wee heck at her nose, and the cow was as healthy as could be and so was the calf!

He turned round and told his wife, "Look, there's only one explanation," he said, "there's only one explanation and you know as well as me . . . there was nobody on this island when me and you left."

"I know," she said to him, "Angus, there was nobody here when we left."

He said, "There's only one person responsible for this."

She says, "I know."

He says, "That was the Broonie."

And that man spent all his days on that island, till he became an old man when he retired to Campbeltown. He believed, and he was a man of the cloth, nobody in the world could convince him otherwise—it couldn't have been anybody but the Broonie who tied up his wee cow that night on the island of Carra. And that's the last of my wee story!

———

This is a wee story that was told to me by a friend of mine way back in Argyll many many years ago, and he told me that this story was true.

———

[2]*heck*—a wee wooden press for holding hay that comes out above the cow's neck so it can stand and chew, and eat a wee drop at a time

Saltie
the
Silkie

I t was this man, his wife, and two grown-up sons, the couple had married very young and bought this old boat. The man sailed from island to island and he kept to the coastline— very very seldom he ever was on the road except maybe he would pitch his tent and stay at the shoreside in the winter months when it was too rough to sail. But otherwise his wife and him and his two sons always stayed in the water with the boat . . . it was a good size o' boat, and it took three folk to handle it, like the father and the two sons.

So one day the mother, who wasn't too old a woman even though she had grown-up sons, had a wee girl, a baby. And it was only a couple of days old when it died. Naturally in these days the travelling folk didn't register the weans as they do nowadays; they just went and had a wee ceremony, buried it by the shoreside. And the woman was very very sad at losing her baby—she always wanted a wee girl—she was so upset.

So they had their wee sermon as travelling folk really do, packed their tent stuff in the boat, and away they sailed. They sailed along slowly, the boys were rowing the boat and the old man was taking a rest up in the front, the woman was sitting at the back. They were sailing along quite naturally when the woman looked over the back of the boat—there coming towards them was a wee baby seal, it was sailing along in the tide quite close behind the boat. So she reached out, lifted it in, and saw it was only about two or three days old. And the man saw her lifting it.

19

He said, "Woman, what are ye gaunna do wi that?"

"It's a wee baby seal," she said, "it's lost. It's prob'ly lost its mother."

"Well, put it back," he said, "in the water."

"No," she said, "I'm gaunna keep it for a pet."

So after her losing a baby the man didn't want to upset her too much. "But, wumman," he said, "it'll mebbe be days before we come to a fairm or a croft along the shoreside afore ye can get milk for it. And it'll die wi ye anyway."

She says, "I've got plenty milk—o' my own." The woman was after losing her baby and she had plenty of milk in her own breasts.

"Ye canna dae that," the man says to his wife.

She says, "I'm gaunnae dae it, and I'm keepin it for a pet."

So, not to disturb her anymore, "Well," he says, "please yoursel. But if onything bad happens tae ye ower the heid o' it, blame yoursel. Ye ken what these kind o' beasts is." He said, "Woman, that's no a wean, that's a seal."

She says, "I know it's a seal, it's a baby seal. And I'm takin it and I'm keepin it! I'm gaunna feed it." So she turned her back to her man and her two sons, she held the baby to her breast and suckled the baby seal. So it was quite contented after having a good drink, it went to sleep. She rolled it in a shawl and she put it *in her oxter*[1] like a baby.

So that night they docked their boat on the shoreside, and the man put up his tent as usual. The two sons went and got plenty of firewood and went for water, did everything that they needed done. She said nothing, she sat on a rock with the baby seal rolled in a shawl.

And her man came to her. "Woman, look," he said, "I know that you lost your baby and I'm sorry for ye, but you're jist makkin too much o' that animal."

She said, "It's my animal and it's my pet and I'm gaunna keep it."

---

[1] *in her oxter*—under her arm

So she kept it, she fed it and took care of it, looked after it. She had the seal for two or three months and the seal grew up, became a young pup and followed her every place she went. Naturally, when the man got accustomed to the seal and saw it was all right, he paid no more attention to it. And the two sons liked it as much as their mother liked it, but it wouldn't have anything to do with them, never came near them. It wouldn't go near the man either, but it loved the woman just like a pup.

Well they sailed round all the coast, they made baskets, made tin, and they hawked the houses. Wherever she went, the seal went with her, she wouldn't leave it any place. At night-time she used to take it down to the sea and teach it, put it in the water and it would go away swimming, it would play itself in the water and it always came back to her. Well, she had that seal for about six months—it was nearly half grown—till she couldn't hardly lift it, it was getting that big. Now it could go and fend for itself in the sea, and it always came back to her.

So one evening, it was the middle of summer and a lovely evening, they docked their boat on the shoreside. And the old man and the laddies put up the tent. The woman thought she'd take down her seal to the shore as usual, it having been in the boat all day, and give it a swim. So she took it down, put it in the water, and away the seal went. It swam away out, it swam out—she kept shouting to it but it wouldn't come back—and then it disappeared. She waited and she waited, she waited for hours and she shouted and waited, but the seal never came back. It disappeared. She went back up to the tent, couldn't rest, she couldn't do anything she was so worried about her seal. She told her man about it.

"Ach, woman," he said, "it prob'ly got fed up wi yese, mebbe it's away back tae its ain folk anyway." That's what he said, "back tae its ain folk."

So even the laddies tried to tell their mother, "Look, Mother, ye canna keep it onyway, because someday when it

gets too big it has to go away, it's got to take care o' itsel!
Ye've done the best ye could for it, reared it up noo to take
care o' itsel, so the best thing you could do is let it go."

But this wouldn't content the old woman. After teatime she
went back down again to the shoreside, and she had a good
wee bit to walk from where the camp was to the shore where
she'd put the seal. You could see the smoke of the camp but
you couldn't see the camp. But when she came down to where
she'd put the seal away, there sitting on the rock was the
bonniest wee lassie she'd ever seen in her life—about eight or
nine years old! She was sitting with her bare feet, dabbling
with her feet in the water.

The woman went up and she said, "Hello, dearie, where do
you come fae?"

"Och," she says, "I cam *away a long way.*"[2]

"But I've never seen any houses or any crofts," the woman
said to her, "or any farms along the shore."

"No, no, I cam a long way from here," she says, "a way
along the shore."

"And," she says, "what are you doin?"

"Och, I'm just playin' mysel." She says, "Where do *you*
come fae?"

"Oh," she says, "me and my husband and the two boys
has got a tent along there, we have a boat and we sail on
the sea."

She said, "Could I see your tent?"

The old woman said, "What's about your people, your
parents? Do they no miss ye, will they no come looking for
ye?"

"No! No, they'll no come looking for me," she said, "I
dinna have any parents, I'm an orphan."

The old woman thought it was kind o' queer. She said,
"Are ye hungry?"

"Yes," she said, "I'm a wee bit hungry, a wee bit."

---

[2]*away a long way*—from a long way off

"Well, come on up to wir fire," she said, "and I'll get ye something to eat. I'll try and get my boys to walk ye home tae where yir people is."

But the wee lassie said, "They cannae walk me home tae my people because my people is miles from here, I don't even know where my people is."

So she took her up to the fire and she told the old man and the two laddies.

The old man was surprised when she came up with this wee lassie. "But, wumman, whaur did ye get the wee lassie?" He said, "You cannae take—"

"I got the wee lassie sittin on a rock," she says, "at the beach where my seal went awa. I went doon callin on the seal and it never cam back, I got this wee lassie sittin on the rock."

The old man spoke to her in cant: "*Shanness, woman, that's hantle's wee kinchen.*[3] Ten chances tae one, her faither's a shepherd or a fairmer along there," and he said they would come looking for her. "And," he says, "we'll get the blame for takkin her awa. Now we'll get intae trouble— we dinnae want to get intae trouble with the *country hantle!*"[4]

The old woman said, "The wee lassie's hungry. She's awfae hungry, gie her something to eat."

So they gave her tea and cakes or bannocks, whatever kind of food they had. The wee lassie was quite content.

And the old woman says, "Dearie, could my boys walk ye home and see that ye'll be safe?"

She says, "I don't have any home! I've nowhere to go to, I don't know how I havena got nae home."

The old *gadgie*[5] says, "Mebbe the wee *gurie's*[6] wandert," meaning "maybe she's lost." He spoke in cant to the woman so's the wee lassie wouldn't understand what he was saying.

---

[3]*Shanness . . . hantle's wee kinchen*—Shame on you . . . that's a child belonging to country folk [4]*country hantle*—non-travellers [5]*gadgie*—man [6]*gurie*—girl

But no, the wee lassie said, "I would like to stay with youse and I would like to go sailin on your boat, I'd love to go sailin."

Now the old woman liked this wee lassie. She said to her man, "If she hasna got nae hantle belongin tae her, mebbe a wee orphan lassie, mebbe we could *bing*[7] her wi us."

"Oh no, shanness," the old man said, "you cannae dae that! Ye canna bing the wee lassie, bring the country folk's wee lassie wi ye, no way can you bring the wee lassie wi ye!"

But anyway, the wee lassie wanted to stay, there was no way they could convince her: she had no place to go.

Now, by the time they were finished talking it over, it was getting dark. The old woman had her own bed in the tent and she said, "Dearie, ye canna go home the night, come in wi me." So the old woman took the wee lassie in with her in bed; she slept beside the old woman all night till the morning.

They got up in the morning, had their wee bit breakfast, and the old man said to the wee lassie, "Dearie, we'll have tae be movin on, we cannae stay here because there's nothing for us here. You sure we cannae take ye . . . ?"

"No," she said, "there's no place I want tae go tae except I want to go wi Mother."

"But, dear," he said, "that's no your mother, ye must have a mother o' your own."

"No, I don't have a mother," she says, "this is all the mother I have and this is all the mother I want!"

They tried to coax her and convince her, but no way. Anyway, by the time they got the boat ready and all their stuff packed into it, the wee lassie jumped in the boat with them.

Away she went with them, and the old woman said, "I'm gaunnae keep her for the wean that I never had in my life, for the lassie I never had—I'm gaunnae keep her."

---

[7]*bing*—take

The old man said, "You're gaunnae get intae trouble, the police'll be after hus, the people'll be lookin for her all over the world and she'll be reported missin and we'll get the blame for stealin her!"

"Tsst," the old woman said, "look, if the police comes and we take good care o' her, we'll give her back and tell them we got her on the beach miles away fae onybody—we thought she was lost and we dinna ken where her folk is."

"Well," the man said, "I'm gaunnae hand her in to the first place I come tae."

"Well," the old woman said, "Okay, we'll dae that."

But they took the wee lassie with them and they sailed from place to place, and from place to place for about six months; there was no word wherever they went to. And the wee lassie loved this old woman like she never loved anybody in her life—she wouldn't even go out of her sight! Wherever the old woman went, the lassie went with her. And the old woman loved this wee lassie like nothing on this earth.

Now this upset the two laddies because the woman had more affection for the wee lassie than she had for them, you see! But the lassie never paid any attention to the man and the laddies, she *cracked*[8] to them and was civil but she never had any time for them.

So when they came beached at night, the old woman said to the wee lassie, "Can you swim?"

"Well, Mother," she says, "I cannae swim but would you teach me?"

So that night after they'd beached the boat on the shoreside, she took the wee lassie well away from the camping place to a nice wee bit on the beach and took her in the water, and showed her what to do—move her hands and kick her feet, showed her how to swim. But she saw that the wee lassie could do it far better than she could tell her!

---

[8]*cracked*—discussed news and gossiped

And then the wee lassie began to swim—"Is this the way you do it, Mother, is this the way?" She began to swim out.

"Come back, dearie, come back," she says, "it's too deep oot there."

And the wee lassie started to dive, to go up and under.

She says, "Ye ken, ye're a good swimmer, wherever ye learned it, ye must hae been able to swim before."

"No, Mother, it just cam tae me right away," she said.

She says, "Ye ken this, ye're a richt wee *saltie*!"[9]

And that was the name the old woman gave her, from that day on she called her "Saltie." But Saltie stayed with them for another six months and she and the old woman were just the greatest of friends. Every day she used to go hawking with the old woman too, selling her baskets and tinware to the houses.

So one day she says, "Mother, dae ye never get fed up on the sea? Dae yese never go on the roads?"

"Oh dearie," she says, "I hev sisters wanderin' the roads and I've never seen them for years, but my man likes the shore and he likes the sea, tae be on his own wi his twa sons on the sea. But my ambition is tae leave the sea, I'm fed up on the sea! I never see a *sowl*,[10] I never see nane o' my ain folk or nane o' my ain family. And I hev sisters and brothers on the mainland, traivellin folk, but I never see them fae day oot and day in."

"Well, Mother," she says, "what would you really like to do, the best thing in yir life ye wad like tae dae?"

"Well, Saltie, what I would like tae dae, is tae pack up this sea-gaun life and," she says, "leave it, go back to the land and live on the land for a while because I'm fed up wi the sea— the salt in my blood!"

"Well," she says, "Mother, we'll hev tae try and do something aboot that for you, won't we!"

---

[9]*saltie*—a sailor, fond of the water   [10]*sowl*—person

Now the two laddies were named Willie and Sandy. About
two or three days later Willie picked up a bit rope he had tied
at the back of the boat to go for a bundle of sticks for the
fire.

When he picked up the rope Saltie said, "Can I come wi ye
and help ye?"

"Well," he said, "Saltie, if ye want to come, you can help
me pack up some sticks." This was the first time she'd ever
been civil to Willie, the first time she'd ever asked to go with
him. So they travelled about two or three hundred yards
along the shore collecting driftwood and putting it in heaps
along the shore. And she was clever at picking up the sticks,
you know—her in her bare feet, never wore shoes!

"Willie," she said, "I hev something to tell ye."

He said, "What is it, Saltie?"

"Ye ken," she said, "your brother disna like you very
much."

He said, "What?"

She said, "Your brother disna like you very much."

So he said, "What makes you think that?"

"Well," she said, "last night while you were awa along the
rocks fishin, I heard him talkin tae your father and he was
tellin him that you were lazy and he's tae dae all the work,
he's tae dae maist o' the rowin o' the boat and everything and
all ye'll dae is go and fish and gather sticks—he's tae dae the
maist o' the work!"

"Oh, is that the way o' it," he says, "is that the way they
dae it when I'm no aboot!"

"Aye," she said, "that's true, but dinna be tellin him I tellt
ye!"

"All right," says Willie, "I'll no say a word about it."

But the next night after they'd beached the boat and put the
tent up . . . Sandy's turn to go for sticks. She went with
Sandy and told him the same thing.

"Oh," Sandy said, "is that the way o' it?"

"I heard your father and Willie speakin aboot you last

night, Sandy. And," she said, "they were sayin' that you were lazy and you didna dae half the work that they dae, and you'll no mak nae baskets, you'll no help your father with the tin and you're lazy—you just sit on the shoreside and wash your feet, ye'll no help nae way!"

"Oh," he said, "is that what they're sayin!"

She said, "They think they wad be better off withoot ye."

He said, "Is that what they think aboot me!"

"Well," she said, "dinna tell them I tellt ye!"

So that night they were gathered round the fire, the two brothers started to argue and started to fight. The old father tried to stop them and they fought each other.

So Willie, the oldest one (he'd be about eighteen), went to the tent, packed up his belongings, and walked off. He said, "If yese can dae withoot me and I'm no good enough for to stay with youse, I'll go on the mainland and find my uncles."

So the next night after they beached the boat, the old man went for sticks.

Saltie went with him. "Ye ken, Sandy disna like you very much," she said, "he blames you for his brother gaun awa . . ." She told the old man all these stories.

The old man said, "It wasnae my fault, he shouldna be fightin his brother and he wouldna went away in the first place."

"Well," she said, "he blames you! He was tellin me."

"Was he tellin ye?" he said.

"He tellt me and Mother aboot you're the fault o' it," she said, "and he canna row a boat hissel."

When the old man came back, he and Sandy had the biggest argument in the world. ",Well," Sandy said, "if that's the way you feel on't, I'll go on my way, and you can row the boat yoursel!"

The old man said, "Ye canna leave me, I canna row a boat!"

"Well," he said, "if ye canna row a boat, ye can dae withoot a boat! I'm goin into the country to see my uncles. In fact, I'm fed up on the sea onyway, I'm sick o' the sea, I'm goin into the country There's bound to be other places to live as wanderin a sea all the days of your life onyway." He packed his wee bits o' belongings and he went away.

Now there's only Saltie and the man and woman left. So that night she said, "Mother, I want to go for a swim."

"Come on then, Saltie, I'll tak ye for a swim."

So they were sitting down at the shoreside before she went into the water. She said, "Mother, are you worried?"

"Well," she said, "I'm a wee bit worried."

She said, "Are ye worried aboot Sandy and Willie? They're big young men, they'll manage to take care o' theirsel."

"I think," she said, "they'll manage to take care o' theirsel, but what's about their poor father—he'll never in the world row that boat his ain sel because it's far too big for ae body."

"Well," she said, "Mother, that's what ye wantit, isn't it! If he canna row a boat then he'll have to leave it, and if he leaves it, I'm sure you'll hev to go wi him!"

"Saltie, I never thocht that—maybe it's a good thing that Willie and Sandy went awa. If my auld man," she said, "leaves this boat and goes on the land, prob'ly I'll see my sisters and my brothers again, and the laddies if they ever meet up with them."

"I'm sure," she said, "you'll see the laddies again."

"I never thocht, Saltie, aboot that," she said.

"Well, Mother," she said, "I'm gaun for a swim."

So she took off her dress and dived into the water and she swam out, swam out and out, and the old woman waved her back, "Come on, Saltie! It's too deep oot there, you might get yourself intae trouble."

And just like that Saltie disappeared—she had held up her hand and gien her a wave and then she was gone. The old woman waited and waited, she was *greetin and roarin*.[11]

---

[11]*greetin and roarin*—crying and shouting

Up to the old man she went, "That lassie has droont! She's disappeared, she's droont!"

The old man said, "What happened tae her?"

She said, "She went swimmin and she gied me a wave."

"Look," he said, "that was nae lassie, woman. I knew all along, that was nae lassie. Woman, that was a silkie! That was your seal—cam back to repay ye for savin its life. But what I'm worryin aboot noo—hoo am I going to row a boat mysel?"

So the old man left the boat on the shore and rolled his bundle on his back and him and the old woman went on the mainland, never again did he go back to the sea. The old woman met her two laddies later on and all her brothers and sisters, and she told them the same story I'm telling you. But she never forgot Saltie the silkie.

———

This travelling family was unique because instead of walking on the road they sailed on the sea, and people called them "sea tinkers." I heard my father a long time ago speaking about them—there's only supposed to have been one travelling family that sailed, were sea tinkers, I think they were MacAlisters. My old grandfather, he'd remembered them . . . they used to sail through the Crinan Canal, right down, right round all the coast, all the islands; this great old clinker-built[12] boat they had. Aye, he told me the ruins of that boat lay on the shore for years and years and years, till it melted away. The old man walked away and left the boat, they took to the land just as the story said. The silkie split them up so's the old woman could go back to the land, that's the way she repaid her.

———

[12]*clinker-built*—made of interlocked strips of wood, typically Norwegian

The
Taen-Awa

any years ago away on the West Coast in a wee hill farm there lived a farmer and his wife. His father had died and left him the farm and he was just newly married. He didn't remember his mother because she had died years before, but he'd loved his old father. Being left the farm and all alone, the first thing he had done was find himself a wife, this girl in the village whom he'd loved and respected. Alistair and Mary MacLean were their names. They had this farm in the glen and a little money that his father had left him and they lived happily together.

Now up on the hills on the West Coast of Scotland there's not much arable land. But Alistair liked to keep a few cattle and a few sheep, and for the cold winter months he just couldn't buy feed. So he tried to make a wee puckle hay, the best he could possibly make. Anything that looked like it was growing to be hay he would leave, keep the animals off it, and cut it with the scythe in the spring or at the beginning of summer.

But one day Mary said to him, "Alistair, I think I've got to give you good news."

"Oh well," he said, "after a hard day's work I would enjoy any good news—what is it you're gaunna tell me?"

"Alistair, I think, Alick," she said, "we're gaunna have a baby."

"Oh," he gasped, "we're gaunna have a baby are we! Oh, it's the best news you've given me today," he said, "it'll make me work ten times harder this afternoon!" So he put his arms around his wee wife and kissed her.

He sat down and they made up plans what they were going to do. "But," he said, "are you sure?"

"I'm sure," she said, "as sure as can be."

Now Alistair wanted to have a son as much as his father had wanted to have him. But to make a long story short . . . sure enough, they had a baby, a beautiful wee baby boy.

And when Alistair came in and saw the wee boy born beside his wife, he said, "Whit are you gaunna call him?"

"Well," she said, "what do you think I'm gaun to call him? I'm gaun to call him 'Alistair' after you, because you're my husband and we live in this glen, on this farm cut off fra all other people—and two Alistairs in the family is not enough for me!"

But anyway, Alistair was so happy to have a baby son and so was his wife. Time passed by and the baby grew up naturally . . . three months, four months, five months, six months, and by this time it was the end of April. And he was sitting up in the cradle.

Now what did Alistair have in the house but an old-fashioned wooden cradle that had passed down through his family, from generation to generation of the MacLeans for hundreds of years. The cradle had a hood and was made in one bit of solid oak with rockers, whereby the woman could sit and put her foot to it to rock the baby. This cradle was about four feet long with a hood to keep the sun or the light off the baby. And Alistair had always promised himself, someday he would have something to put in it—so finally he had!

But this day, April the thirtieth, he said to his wife, "Mary, I'll have tae cut the *wee puckle hay the day*[3] otherwise we'll no have nothing for the cows in the wintertime." In the hills grass grows but you can't grow good hay. But they had a few cows they kept for milk and he said, "Or mebbe for a stack or two, we'll try and get a stack or two—I'll hev to cut a wee bit o' hay."

---

[3]*wee puckle hay the day*—a small amount of hay today

"But, Alick," she said, "I'll come out and gie ye a wee bit holp."

"It's no cut yet." He said, "I'll cut it today—it's no very high, it's very thin, and I think by the day's sun, if it gets a day's sun, I'll be able tae turn it tomorrow." (They turned it with these hand rakes: you walked along behind where the man had cut the hay, after it had a day's sun, and you turned it with a rake that had a long handle and about fourteen teeth on it.)

"Well," she said, "Alick, I'll come oot wi ye tomorra."

"Okay, but," he said, "what about the baby?"

"Ach, it's nae problem, I'll take the cradle under my oxter and," she said, "I'll come oot. I'll put him beside me."

"Okay," he said, "at'd help me a lot."

So Alistair cut all day with the scythe. It was about two acres and it was a hard job cutting with a scythe, but he finished it. The sun was beating down from the sky and he was tired. He took his scythe and stuck it in an old roan pipe beside the barn; took his stone from his belt (he carried a sharpening stone), shoved it beside the scythe, and walked into the farm-house. His wife had his supper ready, so he sat down to eat.

"Mary, I've had a hard day."

"I know," she said, "Alick, ye've had a hard day, but tomorra will be better for hus."

"But," he said, "ye know, Mary, we need the wee puckle hay for the kye in the wintertime."

"Of course," she said, "we need the puckle hay. It's all right, Alick, tomorra we'll take little Alick in the cradle, he'll be no bother tae me! And I'll turn it while you build it intae wee stacks fir the winter."

But that year they'd cut the hay early in the hill because it was a good spring. He said, "Mary, what is it—what's the date on the calendar?" It was an old fly-beated calendar on the wall.

She said, "Alick, I think tomorra is the first o' May."

"Well, upon my soul," he said, "I have never even remembered as a child wi my father, ever bein able tae cut hay on
the end of April, the first of May, for a long long time. I
remember my father tellin me we've done it earlier but," he
said, "this is early for me, and prob'ly by the time we get it
raked up and gaithert mebbe the second crop'll be fine tae let
out the goats on it, after we get it built up."

"Alistair, I wouldna let it bother ye," she said. "If we get
this little pick o' hay gaithert up before the rain comes and
stacked up wi my help, I think we should manage tae keep the
animals alive fir the winter."

He said, "Mary, thank you for all yir help."

She said, "Tomorra morning we'll go out both together."

Sure enough, the next morning they got up bright and
early. The baby was lying in the cradle, bonnie young Alistair
was lying giggling and kicking his bare feet in the cradle.
They had their breakfast, porridge and milk and tea, scones,
cheese, whatever they had. And the sun was shining, it was a
beautiful day.

She said, "Alick, I'm gaun with ye."

He said, "Ye're sure you can manage?"

"Yes," she said, "my dear, I'm sure I can." So she picked
up the cradle below her oxter.

He walked out, took the rake from the back of the barn, and
said to Mary, "Will ye manage the rake and I'll take the
scythe and gae round the borders, cut whatever's left. You
turn what's ever there."

And wee baby Alistair was lying in the cradle giggling to
himself after he'd had his bottle, after his meal.

Now in the middle of the field was a wee bit hill, nothing
grew on it but flowers, daisies, but no hay. And Alistair had
cut round it with his scythe—it was high up in the middle of
the field, a hilloock or a knowe. So Mary came walking up
with the cradle, she thought the best thing she could do was
walk up the wee knowe and leave the cradle at the top. While
she's turning the hay round the knowe she could look up and

see him in the cradle—if anything happened to the baby she would hear it. So she carried the old-fashioned wooden cradle under her oxter and put it on top of the knowe. Baby was fast asleep; she placed it down.

And you know a man cuts bouts of hay with a scythe, lines in circles. Mary walked round and she's turning the hay. Round she goes and round, and round, right round the field— for about two hours. But all in a moment she hears the baby screaming. She puts down the rake, runs up. There's the baby crying from its heart, *greetin*[4] like it never gret before and Mary'd never had any trouble with the baby since it was born.

She said, "Prob'ly it's wet . . . mebbe something's wrong with it, mebbe it's been stung with a bee or a wasp in its cradle." She sat and she coaxed it. She did everything, checked it all over. But no way in the world—it just cried and cried and cried. It cried so much that Alistair, who was away with his scythe on the other side of the field, stuck the scythe in the ground and walked up.

"Mary, what's wrong?"

She said, "It's Alistair—there's something happened tae him, something's wrong with him."

"Well," he said, "mebbe it's wind, it's something . . . what's wrong wi him? What happened?"

"Well," she said, "I left him there and I was turning round . . . everything was peace and quiet. All in a minute he startit tae cry, he startit tae greet. And I cannae get him settlit, I've checked everything about him but there's nothing seems tae make him pleased in any way."

"Is he hungry?"

"No," she said, "he's no hungry."

But baby Alistair cried so much the mother and father couldn't get any peace. He said, "We'll pack it up fir the day."

---

[4]*greetin*—crying

So Mary took the cradle under her oxter away with the baby in it, walked back to the cottage, checked him every way again. But he still gret, and he swinged and gret and he swinged, *gret and swinged*![5] Alistair came in, washed his face, had his wee bit supper. But the baby still cried. And he rocked the cradle but it was no good. They rocked the cradle, it was no good—no way in this world. They tried their very best. But the swingein went on. It wasn't really crying! It was just "aa-heyn, aa-heyn, au-in." It gret and gret and gret—it wouldn't stop, went on and on and on, put the mother and father to their wits' ends!

They sat up all night, but finally about twelve o'clock when the moon was high, the crying stopped. When the full moon came up on the first of May—it went peaceful, quiet! Oh, they blessed each other and thanked God! They went to bed, fell asleep. But about six o'clock in the morning it started again, the greetin.

"God bless us," he said, "what's wrong wi that wean!"

"I don't know, Alistair, what's wrong," she said, "there's something terrible wrong wi him."

"Well," he said, "we'll have tae get the doctor up."

"Well—" she said.

"Luik," he said, "I cannae stick another night like this. I'm gaun for the doctor."

So he had a *garron*[6] pony that he sometimes put in the shafts to pull his mowing machine. Alistair put his riding saddle on the horse and rode the three miles down the glen to the village, to the doctor's.

The doctor had visited Mary after she'd had the baby. "Oh, what's the trouble?" he asked.

Alistair told him the story I'm telling you: "We were oot doin the hay, we took baby Alistair oot in his cradle and put him on the wee hill. My wife was busy turnin the hay, he startit tae cry. And frae then on, Doctor, we have no peace—no

---

[5]*gret and swinged*—cried and whined (cf. *whinge*) [6]*garron*—highland pony

pleasure in the world. He just greets and swinges and cairries on . . . he's breakin wir hearts! But the only thing was, twelve o'clock at night he stopped. But," he said, "it's terrible: that's only the first day, this morning it was worse. And I'm here, I don't know what tae do."

Doctor said, "I'll come up and see him."

The next morning the doctor, with his satchel in his hand, yoked his gig, drove up the glen in his pony and trap, tied his pony to a tree—never unyoked it because doctors didn't unyoke their horses in these days, they just took the reins and tied them round a tree because they knew they weren't going to stay long. He went in. He looked at the baby, checked it, turned it over, stripped it, examined it, sounded it every way in the world. The baby was perfect.

The doctor said, "I cannae find no complaint with it, no way."

She said, "Doctor, is there no something you can—"

He said, "No, *the're*[7] nothing."

And it was still *girnin*,[8] still greetin.

Doctor said, "Nope . . . ," *skelped*[9] its bottom, checked its legs, checked its knees, did everything in the world with it. "I can find no complaint with it in the world," he said, "it's perfect in every way."

"But, Doctor," she said, "luik, cuid ye no stop it, give it something tae stop it fae greetin?"

It wasn't really greetin, it was swingein, going, "A-hung, eh-heng, a-hayn." And this was more upsetting than really greetin. The mother gave it the papppy, she gave it the breast, she gave it the bottle, tried everything—but no way could she content it. It went on and on, for day out and day in.

Now, they didn't have much correspondence with the outside world being up on the wee hill farm, they didn't write many letters or get many visits from other people. But now and again, the old postman used to come up and tell them if

---

[7] *the're*—there is   [8] *girnin*—fretting peevishly   [9] *skelped*—slapped

there was a sale or a market on in the village. The postman used to cycle his old bicycle up the glen and come to Alistair's farm, have his tea there and a crack to Alistair and Mary, because he'd known them since they were children.

So this day, after a couple of weeks had passed by and Mary and Alistair were so very exhausted with their baby they didn't know what to do—they loved it dearly from their hearts—who should happen by? They're sitting down and the baby's sitting in the cradle, with Mary rocking him by the fire, when who had come up but the old postman! A knock came to the door.

Alistair said, "Who's at the door?"

"Och, it'll be the postman," she said, "it's just about his time." So Mary went to the door and she brought the old postman in.

He sat down . . . and the natural thing was for Alistair to give him a dram, because they always kept a bottle of whisky for visitors.

"I cam up, Alistair, tae tell ye," he said, "there's a big market tomorra in the village and there's a lot o' sheep and cattle and goats and hens and everything gettin sellt. So I thought prob'ly that you would maybe be interested."

"Och-och, you know fine, Postie, I'm always interested," he said. "But we have a problem."

"Ach," he said, "what's yir problem?"

"Well," he said, "it's the baby, young Alistair. Ever since Mary and me has been cuttin hay, a queer thing has come over him: he disna stop swingein and greetin. We canna have no peace, we're just put to the world's end with him—and we had the doctor up and everything, he says he cannae find no complaint!" And the baby's lying in the cradle still swingein and greetin!

When the postman went over to him the baby looked up . . . the postman took a long look at him, pulled the blanket right back and stared at the baby . . . he had his own ideas about children. He looked at the baby's face and the blue eyes. But the thing that was interesting to the postman was the baby's skin—on its face the skin was as old as leather, old as leather! Mary and Alistair had never paid attention to this, but the postman thought it was kind of queer. *"I doubt,"*[10] he said to himself, *". . . something queer here."*

Alistair said, "I would like to go to the market, Postie, I wad love to go to the market, but there's no way in the world we can get going. Mary is needin to go to the village anyway, but what can we do: we cannae lea young Alistair here, he greets and swinges so often—there nothing in the world I can do!"

The postie said, "Well, tell ye the truth, I'm no very busy tomorra, the day o' the market. In fact, it's my day off, and if ye wad like tae go, you and Mary, tae the market I'll come up and take care o' the baby while you're gone."

"Oh," Alistair said, "wad ye do that? It'd be just out of this world fir tae let hus off tigether for one day! We've never had a day off for over a year and Mary wants to buy some things fir hersel, and I wad love to go tae the market. If you could take care o' the baby, we'd make it worth your while."

The postman said, "Luik, I'm no needin—you're my friends—I dinna need any money, I dinna want nothing. I'll take care o' the baby while you go to the market, I'll be up tomorra bright and early!"

But the swingein and the greetin still went on. Mary sat and sat and she rocked the cradle, she rocked the cradle till midnight! At last, when the old *wag-at-the-wa clock*[11] in the cottage struck twelve o'clock—quiet, peace for the night.

"Thank my God," she said. "Thank God at last fir peace." So she put him to sleep, crawled in beside her husband, and the both of them fell asleep with exhaustion.

But in the morning, six o'clock, when the cocks on the farm crowed, the swingein started once more. Mary got out of her bed in her nightgown, ran down the stairs and she tried her

---

[10] *I doubt*—I suspect [11] *wag-at-the-wa clock*—pendulum wall clock

best: bottle of hot milk, cuddled it, kissed it, broke its wind, did everything—no, the girnin and swingein still went on. But between the girnin and the greetin and Mary's shaking the cradle, Alistair had got up because he had to go to the market. The two of them were upset about what they were going to do.

She said, "Dae ye think it's safe tae leave it with the old postman, dae ye think he can keep it quiet?"

"Well, Mary," he said, "we've had an awfu time o' it fir the last three weeks and fir a month and . . . luik, I hev tae get to the market and you hev tae get to the village for the things ye need. And if he's gaunna greet with hus, he's gaunna greet wi the auld postman tae, so what's the difference?"

They were sitting discussing it when a knock came to the door, here was the old postie with his old bike up from the village.

"Good morning, people, good morning! It's a nice bright morning," the old postie said, "a lovely day fir the market."

"Oh," Alistair said, "it's a lovely day fir the market but it's no a very lovely day for hus."

"Well, tae tell ye the truth," he said, "I've cycled up the glen this morning tae see youse young people and I want yese tae take yir pony and yoke yir gig, gae doon to the village, and enjoy the market! I'll take care o' the bairn! If it greets wi you, it'll greet wi me—I'll rock it tae sleep, I'll rock it," said the old postie.

The postie's name was Old John. Mary said to him, "Luik, John, ye'll no need tae want for nothing, ye ken where the cupboard is and ye ken where the food is. If ye get hungry, help yoursel tae onything ye need!"

"This is my day off," he said, "and I want youse two tae enjoy yousel," because they were his friends and he loved the young couple very much. "Dinna worry about the bairn!"

Now Alistair had cut his corn, a wee *puckle*[12] oats he had,

---

[12]*puckle*—small amount

and he'd built a corn stack out in front of the farm. After cutting the hay three months had passed by, now it was August. And Alistair always grew a wee field of corn to feed his beasts. He'd gathered it up and built a wee stack right in front of the farm on his stackyard, the hay and the corn were up. Now they had suffered the swingein and greetin for nearly four months but still they'd managed to get on with their work.

"Now I want youse two young people," said the old postman, "tae forget about young Alistair, forget about the farm, forget about me—I'll take care o him."

Mary says, "You're sure ye'll be all right?"

Alistair says, "I'm terrified tae go and leave ye."

He says, "Luik, get your pony and trap and get to the village!"

They were kind o' *sweerin*[13] to go, but the old postman, old John, finally coaxed them to go to the market. Anyway, they were a wee bit relieved to get away for a wee while. Alistair yoked the pony, the garron horse, into the trap and he and Mary got in, bade good-bye to old John.

As he shook the horse on, Alistair shouted, "Mind and take care o the bairn!"

He said, "Dinna worry—I'll be here aa day!"

So they had a big fire, it was all peats they burned. Old John pulled the cradle up beside the fire and he lay back. He stretched out his foot and began to rock the cradle. But the swingein and greetin is still going on in the cradle. Old John is sitting rocking the cradle, "I wonder upon my sowl, what's makkin ye greet so much—there must be something wrong with you—you're in pain."

But then all in a minute a head popped up! And the baby sat up, pulled the white shawl off its head. Beautiful silver hair it had, blue eyes—but the skin was old and sallow-looking on its face.

---

[13]*sweerin*—reluctant

It said, "John!"

"What, what—" John said, "what, whit-whit—are ye talkin?"

"John," he said, "are they gone?"

And the postman was amazed at this.

He said, "Are they gone, John?"

"Aye," he said, "are ye talkin aboot yir father and mother?"

"Aye," he said. "How long have they been gone?"

"Oh," he said, "they'll be well doon the glen by noo."

"Well," he said, "I've got time noo, I can get oot o' this."
And he got up out of the cradle! Nappy round his middle and
the bare legs—he pulled the nappy back so he could walk—
and the long silver hair hanging down his back: up out of the
cradle, he walked across the floor. He was only about three
feet high.

And old John stood up. He was shocked. "Wh-wh-what am
I gaunnae dae? What—"

"You dae nothing," he said, "listen, wheesht! Wheesht,
you dinna ken nothing! You dinna ken a thing—you cam up
here today tae take care o' me, luik—I'm gaunna take care o'
you! But mak me one promise, ye never breathe a word o'
what happens in this hoose!"

Up he goes, with his baby-bowed legs, travels to the cupboard; out with the bottle of whisky, out with two glasses.
Guggle, guggle, gugug, fills the glass.

"Noo, John," he said, "drink that up!" Guggle, guggle,
guggle, fills a glass to himself, flings it back. "Aye, they
think," he says, "they're away tae the market today tae enjoy
theirsel."

The old postie's sitting, he's mesmerized, amazed, he doesn't
know what to do! He doesn't know what to say—dumbfounded!

But after he gets a glass of whisky down, the wee baby puts
the bottle down on the floor and says, "Look, this is for me
and you, we're gaunnae finish this—me and you."

"But," John says, "look, you're a baby."

"Aye, they think I'm a baby! But," he says, "I'm no a baby
ataa."

"Ah," old John says, "no. You're no a baby, no, no way. You're no a baby, no way in this world."

He says, "Are ye fir another drink?"

"Aye," says the old postie. Now the postie began to get a wee bit het up by this time.

Another glass to the old postie, one to himself. "Aye," he says, "I bet ye they're enjoyin theirsel in the market noo. Oh, prob'ly he'll be buyin cattle and buyin sheep and aa these things, and she'll be spendin her money in the market. But, humph—they better enjoy theirsel because they're no gaunna enjoy theirsel tonight when they come hame!"

"But whit is it," John said, "what's the problem?"

He said, "It's no my problem, it's their problem. They took me oot and left me in the hill, lying by my lane while they cut the hay. I lay by mysel and they never gied me a thocht, and that's why they're gettin punished the day."

But old John had his own ideas. He said to himself, "That's nae, that's nae wean—they've nae idea."

"But," he said, "that's no the start o' it . . . He's got a stack o' corn oot there. Go on and get me a corn strae!"

"Wean," John said, "wean, what are ye gaun tae do?"

He said, "Luik, are ye wantin something tae drink or are ye no wantin it?"

And the old postie was *well on*[14] now, the old postie would do anything.

He said, "Go oot and pick a big corn strae oot o' the stack. Pull a big ane!"

"But, wean," he said, "what are ye gaun tae dae wi a corn straw?"

He said, "You go and get me a corn strae oot o' the stack. It's only oot the door there, my faither's stack across the door—noo get a big corn strae!"

Poor old postie, he was upset, he didn't know what to do. But to please this wean—he didn't know, was it a wean or

---

[14]*well on*—under the influence of alcohol

what it was— and him being well on with drink, the best thing he could do was do what the wean told him. So he walked out and he walked round, all round the wee sheafs of corn on the stack till he saw a wide straw and he pulled the big straw out. It was half an inch wide, he pulled it in with the heads of corn on it. He came back in. It's sitting with its legs crossed at the fire and the bottle between its legs, the nappy round its bottom, the long silver hair hanging down its back, and the blue eyes and the old-fashioned skin on its face. Poor old John, he was so mesmerized he didn't know what to do.

"Did ye get it?" said the wean.

"Aye," he said, "I got it."

"Well," he said, "gie it tae me!"

He took a poker, rammed it in the fire, and made the poker red hot. He took the corn straw, measured about eight inches— the best bit of the straw—and he broke it off, flung the rest in the fire. He squeezed the top of it flat to make a reed. When the poker was hot, he took it out of the fire and bored six holes down the straw, turned it around and he bored a hole at the back. And old John's sitting watching him, the old postman never saw anything in his life like this.

"Upon my sowl," he said, "and upon my God, this is nae wean! This is a fairy, this is a fairy," the old postman said to himself. He never said it out loud! "This is a Taen-Awa! Upon my sowl, a Taen-Awa!" (A Taen-Awa means "a baby that was taken away with the fairies.")

Now he's sitting cross-legged with a bottle between his legs and he said to the old postie. "How're ye feelin?"

The postie said, "I'm feelin all right."

"Well, come on," he said, "we'll finish the bottle, the're plenty mair in the cupboard," and he gied the postie another glass. "Drink that up, John! But we dinna hae much time tae waste because it'll no be long till they're back. But," he said, "afore they come back, I'm gaunna play ye a wee tune. Brother, I love music! I love music frae my hert!"

He got the corn straw in his hands with the seven holes bored into it, and he started to play—the jigs and reels and jigs and reels that you never heard in your life before. And the old postie was lost, he didn't know where he was, was he coming or going! Now the postie's half drunk.

And the postie said, "Go on, wean, go on, wean, go on, wean—play on!" The postie's drunk now. And the wean's playing the corn straw, the jigs and reels. The postie liked music himself. And he's playing all this music from the corn straw that you never heard before in your life. No way in the world did the postie ever hear music like this from a corn straw!

And the time passed by. When all in a minute the music stopped. He caught the corn straw and flung it in the fire, jumped back in the cradle. "They're hame!" He lay back, pulled the blanket over him, put the *cool*[15] back on his head— "Eh-hee, oo-hoo, u-hung."

And then the door opened, in came Màry. She was carrying bundles and parcels and things in her oxter. "Oh, John, I'm sorry," she said, "John."

"Hay-heng," it's lying greetin in the cradle.

She says, "I'm sorry, John, to put wir troubles upon ye. I ken ye didnae hae much enjoyment."

"Oh no," he said, "I didna hae nae enjoyment!"

But by this time Alistair had loosened the pony out, taken off the harness, put the pony in its stable, and come in. He had a bottle of whisky in his hand. "For bein so kind, John, I brought you a wee dram."

And there was the postie sitting well on with drink.

"Would you like a wee drink, John?" he said.

"Well, Alistair, tae tell ye the God's truth, no." He said, "Luik, I've had enough."

"Oh," he said, "you've been helpin yoursel."

"No, I've no been helpin mysel, but," he said, "wait a

---

[15]*cool*—cowl, hood

minute. . . . Can I talk tae ye a minute, you and your wife?"

And this thing's lying in the cradle and its girnin, it's greetin and it's *woein*,[16] greetin and girnin. And when it heard these voices it roared harder and harder and harder!

The postman said, "Stop!"

She said, "How did ye get on wi young Alistair?"

"Luik," he said, "let it greet. Come here, I want tae speak tae ye, let it greet—let it go on greetin for evermore. Come into the other room."

But Alistair said, "What's the trouble, what's the bother? Did it give ye so much trouble?"

"It gied me nae trouble," he said, "Alistair, it gied me nae trouble. It gied me a drink and it gied me the best music I ever heard in my life, frae a corn strae!"

Alistair said, "John, you must be drunk."

"No, I'm no drunk. Come intae the other room." So the postie took them into the other room and he told them, "Luik, Mary and Alistair, I want tae tell you something: I'm no drunk, but I've had a few drinks . . . That in your cradle is a Taen-Awa."

And Alistair said, "What's a Taen-Awa?"

And Mary said, "What's a Taen-Awa?"

He said, "When you took your baby oot to the hill tae cut the hay and put it on a knowe, the fairies took your wean and put that thing in his cradle. That played tae me like I never heard music before in my life, that sat and shared a bottle o' whisky wi me!"

And Alistair said, "Ye're crazy, man!"

"I'm no crazy, Alistair, listen," he said. "That is no your wean, that is a Taen-Awa in yir cradle!"

He finally convinced him that it was a Taen-Awa. "But what're we gaunna do?" Alistair said. "What are we gaunna do then?"

---

[16]*woein*—being sad, lamenting

He said, "I'll tell ye what ye're gaunna do: there's only one way that you're gaunna get rid o' that and get yir ain wean back. Kid on you don't know what I tell ye! Have you got a new shawl, Mary?"

"Aye," she says, "I bocht one today for to wrap it in."

"Well," he says, "wrap it in the new shawl and pit its hands doon between its legs, wrap it up as ticht as ever ye can get it. But don't let its hands oot, no way in this world! And I'll come wi ye, and," he said, "Alistair, you come tae!"

"But," Alistair says, "what are ye gaun tae dae wi it?"

He says, "A water *clift*!¹⁷ The clift—the waterfall is the only answer." (There was a river running by the farm that was close by. A wee *burn*¹⁸ dropped about fifty feet over to a pool. The fish couldn't jump it because it was too steep. Alistair used to fish the pool in his own time for trout.) He says, "Look, Mary, there's only one cure for it, if ye want tae get rid o' that thing that's in the cradle—that's nae wean, that's a fairy! A fairy took your wean's place. I'll stay wi ye the night and we'll take it to the clift. Wrap its hands ower very carefully because when you tak it there," he says, "if it gets a grip o' you and takes ye wi it, you'll never be seen again in a million years. If its hands even touches ye, you'll go wi it ower the clift—and you're the only one that can fling it ower the clift."

"But God bless my sowl and body," says Alistair, "why should such thing happen tae the likes o' hus?"

"Well," says the old postman, "this is no something new, this has happened tae many people, long ago."

"But hoo," says Alistair, "in the world did you ken aboot this?"

He says, "My granny tellt me: there's only one way tae get

---

¹⁷*clift*—cliff   ¹⁸*burn*—a small stream

rid o' a Taen-Awa—fling it ower a clift wi its hands tied
between its legs."

"But," Mary says, "it's my baby, I dinna want tae fling
it."

He says, "That's no yir baby, that's a greetin swinge that's
in there. It played the pipes tae me and gied me whisky.
Dinna ye believe me? It sat and drank a bottle o' whisky wi
me, it played a corn strae tae me—that's nae wean! That's a
fairy!"

So the old postman finally convinced them that it was a
fairy. "Noo," he said, "the night when the clock strikes
twelve, we'll wrap it up in a new shawl and fling it over the
clift." He finally convinced Alistair and Mary it was really
true.

So they sat and they talked. While they talked the swingein
still went on. John said, "Dinna shake it, dinna rock the
cradle—forget about it, let it be, dinna even touch it, let it
sit." So time passed by. They sat and talked and they cracked
till half past eleven. "Now," he says, "Mary, go and get yir
new shawl."

"Ne-yeh, yen-gay, ae-yengh," it's greetin. She took it and
she wrapped it the way the old postman told her, put its hands
between its legs, wrapped it up in the new shawl as best she
could.

"Noo," says the old postman, "you've got it done?"

"Right," she said and packed it in the cradle.

He said, "Come wi me."

So the old postman, Mary, and Alistair walked. They didn't
have far to go to the wee burn. But the burn made a
waterfall . . .

"Noo," says the old postman, "you're the one that's got tae
dae it. There's naebody—we cannae help ye." He says to
Mary, "You tak it, walk tae the top o' the fall, and fling it
doon the waterfall!"

"But," she says, "I-I-I canna—I hate tae dae it, John, I
might never see my wean again."

He says, "If ye want tae see yir wean again, ye dae what I'm tellin ye!"

But the old postman had convinced her. She took it to the waterfall and Alistair came with her and old John went with her right to the face of the cliff. She took it and she flung it over—it fell down the waterfall, and when it hit the pool it stopped, and the shawl opened. It came out, spun on the top of the water. It looked up and shook its fist. "Ye finally found the answer, but," it said, "many's the night when I lay in yir bosom and cuddled ye, I cuid have done terrible things to you—*curse* upon you! And curse upon your old postman!" Like that—he was gone. Gone, disappeared for evermore.

"Come on," said the postman, "that's hit, that's it finished."

So they walked back to the cottage, opened the door, walked in. There was the cradle, and John looked in.

He said, "Look, Mary, in your cradle," and there lying in the cradle was the bonniest wee baby . . . his blue eyes . . . lying smiling up at his mammy. He said, "There, Mary, there's your true baby."

Alistair said, "How in the world, John, did you ken these things?"

"Well, it's on'y grannies' cracks," he said, "and grannies' stories . . . and if ye canna believe me and what I'm tellin you right noo, gang and get the bottle—let's hae a drink!"

So Alistair and the old postman went and got the bottle. They sat and they drank, they finished the bottle. And that is the end of my wee story.

———

My mother's mother, old Bella MacDonald, was a legend in Argyll—still is to this day. Nobody would turn Bella Mac-Donald from their door when she came hawking, because they thought it was bad luck to turn old Bella away. She was like a fairy! She was small and was so kind-hearted she had a pleasant word for everybody. I mean, if she went to some-body's door and they did turn her away, she would say, "God

bless you, missus, and thank you very much for your kind-
ness," and walk away without spite . . . she was an angel to
this world!

Everybody loved Granny. She was about four feet two, and
couldn't wear boots but wore wee children's sandals on her
feet. She wore this old long black apron and a shawl over her
shoulders and two big plaits down her back—she was like a
wee Indian maiden. Her face was just a bundle of wrinkles
and two blue eyes looking out at you! She was a beautiful
wee creature.

Her son, my Uncle Duncan, stayed with his mother all the
days of his life. After travelling Perthshire and before the
long cold winter months set in each year, he'd say, "Granny,
I think the best thing we can do is mak wir back to Furnace
tae your dochter Betsy and Johnnie. At least we'll have a
good place to stay, auld wumman, and you've got a bing o'
friends in Argyllshire." Uncle Duncan could bring her back
there and my father, being lonely, with about sixteen weans
and just my mother to talk to, welcomed his brother-in-law.
Father would say, "Okay, Dunkie, we'll just lift the side o'
the barrikit,[19] brother. I'll pit yir wee tent for you and Granny
aside the barrikit." So he opened the main tent, which was as
big as a large living room, drew a couple of sticks aside, and
built Duncan's wee tent. Oh, he made a good job of it—
covers and everything. It was just another room added to the
kitchen. We used the same fire and Granny was happy to be
back with her daughter Betsy; now she had her daughter, she
had her son and all her grandbairns. She had her pipe and
could sit by the fire and crack.[20] My daddy always kept a big
fire in the middle of the tent, just on the ground. But there
was no drink, no, no drink. It was too hard to get food, never
mind money for drink.

When the dark winter nights came and she had her wee

---

[19]barrikit—a large dome-shaped traveller-made dwelling (See the Introduction to my
Fireside Tales, p. ix.)   [20]crack—tell stories

tent in the barrikit, Uncle Duncan would tell stories past the common and Daddy would tell a story. My mother would tell a crack and then—"Come on, Granny, tell us a story!" There were fifteen or twenty of us in there, but we weren't strangers, we were all our own family and she felt happy— she was home.

But anyway, that was the story, how much happiness we had. We were poor, really poor, we'd had hungry times. But you believe me, we had some good times too. It was really good—what we wanted in one thing we gained in another, see what I mean, we couldn't lose. We had our granny whom we loved so much, we had our uncle whom we loved so much, and we had our father and mother to tell us stories. Food isn't everything in the world; that's all we really looked for. We didn't pay any rent or need any electricity, we just bought a bottle of paraffin for the wee crusie lamp hanging inside the barrikit, which gave enough light for everybody.

This story was my granny's favorite—I hope you enjoyed it. I've told "The Taen-Awa" the way Granny told it to me way back in Furnace in 1935. It wasn't the first time I'd heard it because my daddy told it to me too, when I was younger—I was seven when I heard Granny telling it. But even my daddy enjoyed old Bella's version, it was different altogether from his. She was a good storyteller and came from a line of storytelling folk who went back many hundreds of years, because the MacDonalds were famed for their tales, they really were.

This is what you would call an "international tale" among the travelling folk; every traveller I have met in my travels across Scotland has this story. Some call it "The Banshee," some "Johnnie who Gret." And the thing is, within the same family a brother and sister-in-law or two cousins may each have their own different way of telling the story.

Torquil Glen

here once lived a shepherd and he had a farm away up on a hill in Torquil Glen on the West Coast of Scotland. This shepherd owned this farm and he and his wife had hundreds of sheep. He always took care of the sheep, and the wife used to help him in the summertime to clip them. Days passed by and years passed by, then they had a wee son, a wee boy.

But the shepherd had only one thing that troubled him. From his farm to the village was a large glen, going down the glen was a river and across the river was a bridge, from the bridge there were three or four steps going down to a deep pool beside the water, and no one could ever explain *who* had built the steps going down to this pool!

Now in these days, long gone by, there were no motor cars of any description. The shepherd-farmer used to go to the village with a pony and cart and he used to take his wee son with him. But when he came to the bridge, and the steps, he used to put the whip to the horse, hurry it past!

And the wee son used to say, "Daddy, why is it when you come to the bridge that you always push the pony past? I'd like to see the bridge and I'd like to see the river, I would like to see the steps going to the pool."

"Son," he said, "wheesht! You don't know what I know . . . the Broonie lives in there! And these are his steps, he is in that pool—that's why I hurry the horse past them. You watch it, son, if he ever gets his hands on you, you're finished!"

This went on year out and year in every time he went to

the village. Now the son got this idea in his head that the Broonie was a terrible being, and he owned this bridge, owned the steps going down to this big pool beside the river. The son grew up with this terrified notion that the Broonie was going to do him some harm. His father hated the bridge, he hated the steps, and he hated the pool. The son grew up to be the same way, he had the same idea.

But naturally, when the son came about seventeen or eighteen years of age, the old father died. And the mother died. He buried his father and he buried his mother, and was left with a big sheep farm to himself. He had everything left to him.

And naturally, as time passed by, the son got married to this beautiful girl. He took her home to the sheep farm with him up this glen and they were very happy. But once a week he used to go to the village to collect the messages with his pony and trap. And when he came to the bridge he put the whip to the horse, galloped past as fast as he could because his father had told him that the Broonie was below that bridge. He was terrified. There's no way in the world when nightfall came would that son go down that glen. Through the day he would beat the horse to get it past the bridge, but for nobody in the world would he go down that glen at night-time!

But anyway, there came a time . . . when one night he came in from his work and his wife said to him, "I'm very sick."

He said, "What's wrong?"

"Ye have to go—down the glen," she said.

"But it's night-time, it's dark, I canna gae doon the glen, it's evening, look! Ye see this glen, the Broonie's at the fit o' the glen," he said, "in the pool. And my faither swore he comes oot at night-time!"

"Look, John, you must go!" she said. "It's either the Broonie or me."

He said, "What's wrong wi you?"

She said, "I'm gaunnae have a baby."

"What!" he said.

"I'm gaun to have a baby," she said, "and if I don't have help I dinna ken what's gaunnae come of me. I'm very sick. I'll have to go and lie doon."

Oh John, he scratched his head, he didn't know what to do. Now he's got to yoke the horse, go down the glen, pass the bridge, pass the Broonie's pool—he's terrified of the Broonie and he's so in love with his wife—he wants to go for the doctor but . . . he doesn't know what to do.

He goes out to the stable. And he puts the harness on the horse but he doesn't yoke it. He lights the lamp and he hangs it up inside the stable. When all in a minute in comes an old man through the door, an old gray tramp with a long white beard.

"Hello!" the old tramp said.

John jumped—"Oh, oh what is it?" he said. "What is it?"

The old tramp said, "I'm sorry, I dinna want to disturb ye. I see you're a busy man, I dinna want to bother you."

"What is it you want?" he said.

"Oh, I'm an auld tramp man. I thought," he said, "you would maybe put me up and gie me shelter for the night."

John never said anything in the world—he welcomed the old tramp like he would have the king! "You're just the very person I want," he said, "you're the very person." And this wee tramp was about five feet high with a long white beard and long *shune*[1] on him. John said, "Could you help me and I'll help you?"

"Well," the tramp said, "what is it you want?"

"Look, I hev tae gang doon the glen," he said, "the night, and I'm terrified."

The tramp said, "What are you terrified for?"

He said, "I'm terrified of the Broonie."

Tramp said, "The Broonie!"

---

[1] *shune*—shoes

"Oh, I'm terrified o' the Broonie in the glen! And," he said, "if he comes oot when I pass by, he might put a spell on me and I'll never get back again tae my fairm. My faither tellt me hundreds o' times years ago."

"Ach, it's only auld tales," the old tramp said, "dinna worry! Lead me to your house, let me in. I'll watch your wife, laddie, away you go for the doctor to your wife!" he said. "I'll take care o' her till you come back."

John said, "Are you sure?"

"Look, you go for the doctor to your wife!" He said, "Yoke your pony and your cart and drive doon for the doctor. I'll watch your wife till you come back. It's nine miles doon the glen, and," he said, "nothing'll happen tae her till you come back—I'll take good care o' her."

"God bless you, auld man!" says John.

He says, "Sure!"

"I'll have to go, but," he says, "I'll tell you what I'll dae. I'll shut my eyes when I pass the brig."

"You close your eyes," says the old man, "when you pass the brig, that's the best thing you can dae."

So John yokes his horse, drives down the glen, past the bridge, past the pool, past the steps, drives down to the doctor's house. When he lands at the doctor's, oh, he's shaking!

Doctor says, "Come in! What's wrong, John?"

"Well, Doctor, look. It's this way," he said, "my wife is gaunnae have a baby."

"Oh well," the doctor said, "every woman has babies."

"But it's no that, Doctor—" he said, "ye ken—I'm terrified."

He said, "Terrified! A young man like you afraid o' your wife having a—"

"No," he said, "I'm no afraid o' my wife having a baby, Doctor. I'm terrified o' the Broonie in the glen at the bridge when I go back. If he catches me my faither said he'll put a spell on me, I'll never see my wife again!"

"Ach, that's on'y auld wives' tales. Come on," the doctor said, "I'll come wi ye!"

"Doctor," he said, "if I tak ye up in my cairt, that means I hev tae bring ye back."

The doctor said, "Look, I'll yoke my ain pony, an I'll come behind ye so's you'll no need to bring me back."

So John jumped in his cart and the doctor yoked his pony and gig. They drove up the glen right up to the cottage to the sheep farm. They landed up at the hill, pulled into the house. John tied his horse up, never took his harness off it, he ran in to see his wife. Fire was kindling, the house was clean, lights were burning.

He shouted to his wife and ran into the bedroom. "Where'd that auld tramp go? Where did that auld tramp go! He's supposed to be sittin keepin the fire gaun till I cam back." The tramp was gone.

The doctor came in to where the woman was lying in bed, and beside the woman was a wee baby wrapped in a shawl, wrapped in a white shawl. The doctor said, "Why did you call me? You dinna need me."

"Look," the man said, "my wife is sick—she's gaunnae have a baby, that's why I called ye."

"Well, your wife's no sick now," he said. "She has the baby and—"

"John! Do you know who that auld tramp was?" the woman said. "The auld man took care o' me, *he* brought my baby into the world. And he cleaned the baby up, did everything and fixed it for me. And," she said, "there—is the baby beside me. You were terrified o' the Broonie, John. But ye dinnae need to be terrified any more because the Broonie was here while you were gone."

And from that day on till the day that John died and his wee baby son grew up, John was never again afraid of the Broonie. And that's the last of my wee story!

I've never heard this story from anybody but the travelling folk. My father told it to me, then my granny told me a version of "Torquil Glen," and my Uncle Duncan had the same story about this shepherd who was afraid to go down the glen. We stayed in Argyll—my father believed Torquil Glen was across Loch Fyne in Glendaruel. Now my Uncle Duncan believed it was near Glen Lyon above Aberfeldy in Perthshire. But my granny had different ideas, she believed it was near Glen Coe because she was a MacDonald!

Back in 1948 I was visiting old Betsy Whyte in Fraserburgh, she was eighty when I knew her. We had a wee party in her house, and the subject was brought up about fairies and witches and the Broonie. I said, "I'll tell a story," and it was "The Broonie of Torquil Glen."

So Betsy said to me, "You might think that's a story, but my faither used to sing that song."

"Well," I said, "if you ken it as a song, tell hus hoo it goes!"

"I dinna ken, laddie," she said, "I dinna ken the tune very well. But I remember a wee bit o the verse my faither used tae sing . . . laddie, laddie, it's a lang time ago." She told it in rhyme:

> The wife she poked the fire
> And the sparks flew up the lum;
> "Y'll hev tae gang fir the doctor, John,
> For I think my time has come!"
>
> He could lie oot in the hill
> Wi nothing on but his sark,
> But fir aa the gold in the world
> Wad he go doon the glen efter dark!

Excited, I asked Betsy, "Can you no tell me a wee bit mair?"

She couldn't. And search for everymore, ask all the travellers questions, I never found another person who ever told me "The Broonie o' Torquil Glen" was a song.

But not long ago, when the travelling people got round the campfire, they told stories and sang songs. Someone sang a long song, then saw it was too long and the people around the fire were getting a bit fidgety and disinterested. So the singer stopped and told a wee part, sang another part—and I do that myself sometimes with ballads. Probably "The Broonie o' Torquil Glen" was sung in verse as a long song.

The Lighthouse Keeper

he boat put me out on the island, on The Rock, with a wee bit provisions, and the things which were to keep me for three months at the lighthouse. I took these off the boat and they said, "Well, if the weather's good, we'll prob'ly see ye in a couple o' months."

So I gathered all the wee things and put them in the room, I put them all by where I would need them. And I'd been there for a couple of weeks, the weather was kind of rough— really rough. On The Rock there was a path leading down to the shoreside, it was the only way you could get down to the water, the one path on The Rock. But for days and days I sat in the lighthouse, nothing to do but light the lamps and read the papers, no letters or anything coming from anybody. I would be lucky if there would be another boat for a couple of months.

But one day the weather changed. The sun came out and the sea was calm. I was kind of bored sitting and I said, "Ach, I'll take my rod and walk down the path, because the sea's no so rough today. I'll walk down the wee path. I'll maybe catch mysel a couple o' fish and pass away the time." So I took my rod and walked down. The night before was a terrible storm but this morning was calm. I would try and catch a few fish for my tea. But I never got my fly wet.

I was just about to cast it, a yellow seafly to fish sea trout with, when lo and behold I looked beside The Rock and there against the wall among a puckle seaweed was a seal! And it was lying on its side, the waves were hitting it against

The Rock. I could see by the look on it that it wasn't dead.

I had my wellingtons on, which I usually use when I go fishing, for the spray that washes off the rocks. So I walked down, I caught her and I lifted her up. I could see she was still alive, I said to myself, "You've been sick or you've mebbe been caught in a heavy tide last night and you might be ill. Ye've had a bad time o't, little creature. I better take ye up and see if I can do something for ye."

So instead of fishing that day, I laid my rod against the wall, I said, "I'll get you later on." I took the seal and it was still alive, I could see that it had a good bit of life in it! So I carried it up and it wasn't very light, it was nearly a half-grown seal and a female. I carried her up in *my oxters*.[1] I was glad to see something for company because I hadn't a kitten or a pup or even a mouse in the lighthouse. I carried her right up, I soothed her the best I could.

I put her on the bed, she was very sick, ill, as I thought she was. But I looked around her and saw there was no damage attached to her, there wasn't a hurt, no bleeding or anything. "Ach," I said to myself, "she's prob'ly exhausted." She was about six or seven months old. I put her in the bed and happed her up with a blanket. I said, "Keep yoursel warm there." So I went into the kitchen, I made a drink of condensed milk and fed her with it.

She drank the milk and I said to her, "Little creature, you be quiet there, be kind and stay yirsel, stay there in bed and ye'll be all right because Peter'll take care of ye!" But now by the time I had got her up to the room and given her a drink, evening began to come—evening came very early. I had to go up the stairs to light the lamps. So I left her there in bed by herself after her drink and she was quite contented.

I lighted the lamps, cleaned the reflectors, got the lights set for the evening, and I came down. But by the time I came

---

[1]*my oxters*—both arms

back down she seemed to have recovered a wee bit. Then I went and made a wee bit of supper for myself. I had my supper and came back in, I said, "Are you all right, are you feeling fine now?"

But, och me, God, she was up in bed, she was sitting up fine as could be! Maybe she was a wee bit exhausted. But lo and behold, I had some dried fish and I gave her some, she just gobbled it up as quick as could be. And after she gobbled the fish she seemed to rally as best as could be and I said to myself, "You're not damaged in any way, you're not hurt and not sick . . . you're a good friend and I hope you'll stay with me a long long while." And we began to be good friends.

But lo and behold, I had sat down just for a minute, when she flapped upon the floor. And she flipped and she flapped around the whole place as if nothing had been the matter. I said to myself, "That's kind o' queer." But to me it was exciting just to hear her flippers flapping along the floor. And she went through the whole kitchen, through the whole place, and this "flip-flap" . . . you know, it's very hard when you live in a lighthouse on your own out in the sea and there's not a soul to be seen or not a voice or anybody to speak to or anything, and you're on your own. Even a mouse would cheer you up! When somebody comes flip-flapping around the floor, especially a seal that you have just taken from the sea, it means so much to you—it means the world to you. So I said to myself, "If you're gaunnae flip-flap around the floor as much as that and keep me happy, I'm gaunnae call you 'Flippy.' "

Anyway, I called her Flippy and she flipped around the floor, she was so happy. I fed her the best food I could find. She and I became the best of friends. So after a couple of weeks I said to myself, "That is not just a natural seal. She's so free and so easy that it seems tae me she's been someone's pet or something, that someone had her before. And she's so intelligent." She was just like a puppy to me.

My wife had packed my bag for me that last time I left.

She'd said, "Peter, when you're walking round the light-house, always remember your slippers." So when she'd packed, she'd put my slippers in the bag—instead of putting two slippers in, she put three in the bag. So I had them on my feet, but there's always one left I didn't have a neighbor for. Now in the evenings when the lamps were lighted and after I had my supper, Flippy and I would sit there in the room. I used to throw the one slipper to her. And just like a good dog she would bring it back to me, and I would throw it again. Oh, and this was fantastic, it would pass away the time.

Days passed by. Then one evening I was tired and I lay in the bunk bed. Flippy wasn't very pleased playing with one slipper, but she had to take my other two. So I thought to myself, "Mebbe I could teach her a wee trick or two." So I threw one slipper and she brought it back and left it down, then I threw another and she brought it back and left it down, then I threw another slipper to her, she brought it back and left it down—would you believe it, she left them all in a row! Now this began a game with me and her. Every time I threw a slipper she brought it back. I threw one and another and another, and she'd always bring them back, leave them in a row.

Flippy and I spent three or four weeks together. But I could see that she was longing for something. I said to myself, "Flippy, I know what you're longin for," because sometimes I felt that she felt very sad. One day I said, "I think it's about time I took ye back to the sea tae get back among yir own people." By this time she had grown bigger and I was sad to see her go, sad to part with her. But I carried her down the steps. And there beside the wall was my fishing rod, lying where I'd left it three weeks before.

It took me just bare than busy[2] to carry her down the steps and put her in the water. She swam away, went round two or three times and dived two or three times. She swam out, and I

---

[2]*It took me . . . busy*—she was just enough for me (to carry)

thought she would come back. But I wasn't worried so much because I didn't want to make a pet of her, I knew it would just be ruining her life. She swam for a while. I sat and I cast awhile with my fishing rod. But I never had a bite. I watched Flippy, she circled two or three times, stood up in the water, and then she was gone. And believe me or not, as I'm telling you this story I swear on my mother's grave, she was gone for evermore. I never saw her again.

Now I was kind of sad, but delighted that she was healthy enough to go. I had made her well, and she could go on her own way, because seals need their own people. I took my fishing rod, but I never had any luck that day, so I walked up, and put my rod by in the cupboard. Then the wind began to get up. The storm blew. It blew and I lighted the lamps. I kept inside for a couple of days. And the storm blew harder. For two days I never saw outside the window. But I knew that in another two or three weeks or a month I would be relieved, I would be back with my wife and family. I could tell them the fantastic tale about the seal and how I enjoyed her company. But that would be a long time yet.

Then, about a week later, a terrible thing happened. As you know, I had to walk up the stairs, which are circular, to the lamps. I walked up the steps, I was lighting the lamps, and I opened the window. A gust of wind came straight in after I lighted the lamps, hit me straight in the face. I never knew that the gust was so strong. I stepped back, I slipped, fell, fell down the stairs—three turns down. I couldn't help myself. I hurt my shoulder, hurt my arm, I hurt my head and I'm lying there. I knew that I had made a terrible mistake. I lay there semi-conscious and I knew my arm was broken because I had no feelings in it. I had a terrible bash on my head. I thought to myself, "What's gaun to come of me, because it'll be a week or a fortnight, maybe three weeks"—you lose track of time when you're on your own in one of these lighthouses. I said to myself, "I am not gaunnae survive with this arm, how in the world—when it's broken!"

So I lay in the doldrums, and I would have given the world
if I could have crawled to the room, got myself a wee drink or
something. But I'm lying there in a semi-conscious state
when I heard the flip-flip-flip, flip-flip-flip-flip coming *ben*[3]
towards me. I said to myself, "It's only one person in the
world could make that sound, it must be Flippy has come
back!" I lay there, oh, I was in pain and misery. And I heard
in my mind the flip-flip-flip of the feet on the causeway
coming into the room where I lay. I only had one thought in
my mind, it was Flippy the seal, she'd probably missed me
and come back. She'd be company to me even though I was in
agony.

Then lo and behold, I looked up, and standing beside me—as
sure as I'm here—was a young woman, the most beautiful
young woman I had ever seen in my life. She was standing
there as if she was standing here beside me now, this young
beautiful creature with long dark hair and a tight-fitting dress
on her that you never saw before in your life! Through the
mist of pain and darkness—the light was only shining faintly
from above—I turned round and looked up, I thought I was in
a dream. I said, "My dear, where did you come from?"

And she looked down and said to me, "Are you hurt?"

I said, "Yes, I'm hurt. I fell from the landing, from the
lights. I tumbled down the stairs and landed here. I've hurt
my head and I think my arm is broken."

She bent down and said, "Come and I'll help you."

So she helped me up, and you may believe it or not, she
oxtered me in and put me on my bed. There by the light I had
a good look at her. I saw that she was the most beautiful
creature that I ever saw in my life, with long dark hair and
dark eyes, and this tight-fitting kind of dress on her and her
bare feet. She said, "I'll help you!"

But I said, "In the name of creation, dearie, where in the
world have you come from?"

---

[3]*ben*—further in

She said, "Never mind about me, I'll tell ye about me later. We'll think about you first because you are sick and ill and hurt, and I am not. We'll get you fixed up first."

So believe it or not, she put me in bed, she took off my boots. She took my arm, got it set, she spliced it—a doctor or a specialist couldn't have done a better job. And she bathed my head with water, made me feel comfortable. I lay there in a semi-conscious state believing I was in a dream. But there she was standing before me . . . I finally fell asleep.

I wakened to the flip-flap, flap-flap-flap in the morning. And would you believe me what I'm telling you, you probably won't, but it was the flip-flap of her bare feet on the floor that sounded so much like the flippers of my seal who had gone weeks before.

She sat down on the bed beside me and said to me, "Drink this. This is something that'll make you well." She had a cup in her hand, one of my mugs.

I said, "What is it?"

"Oh," she said, "never mind what it is. Just you drink it, it'll make you feel better."

I was so amazed, I didn't understand—I just drank this to please the young woman, not to insult her. To see a young creature in a lighthouse miles away from the land . . . I was in such a state, I didn't know was I coming or going. But I took the cup from her hand and I drank, the first taste was like seaweed. I've had pieces of seaweed, because in my old father's time along the shores years and years ago, Father used to say that sucking a piece of dry seaweed was good for you. It was full of iron. This stuff in the cup tasted the same, and sure and behold I hadn't drunk it for very long when I felt better, a lot better.

Well, to make a long story short, she tended me all that day and all that night. By the next morning I felt even better and the dizziness in my head was gone. My arm felt a wee bit better. So I sat up in bed and said to her, "Young woman, where in the world have you come from? To come to this lighthouse well away from the mainland is just something that's unexplainable."

"Well," she said, "tae tell ye the truth, I wis out in a fishin party with a few friends and the storm came up. The boat capsized. Everybody swam fir their life and I got lost in the storm, I saw yir light and I swam here. I saw yir lighthouse and I knew I'd find refuge, but I don't know what happened tae the rest of my friends."

I said, "Tae tell you the truth, there's no communication between here and the mainland. The next boat . . . will be weeks before it arrives and the're nothing we can do about it. I'm sorry for your friends, but you're lucky that you managed tae survive."

She said, "I hope they'll survive the same way as me. But in the meantime, if we're gaunnae be here till the next boat comes, we'd better get tae know each other."

"Well," I said, "my name is Peter MacKinnon."

She said, "My friends call me Rona."[4]

"If me and you have tae be here together," I says, "fir the next couple o' weeks—let me see now, it'll be a fortnight anyway before the boat comes again tae relieve me from the lighthouse."

She said, "By that time you should be fit and able tae be on your feet."

But sure enough, the next day I felt ten times better! Och, I felt better than ever I felt in my life, but for this damned arm that was broken! But she'd set it and put a sling around my neck. And I got around the lighthouse, I was doing everything I could with one hand.

So we sat evenings out and we talked of many things, but she would never talk about her people. A week had passed. She cooked for me and tidied up, she did everything for me that I really needed done. And I loved her like nothing on this earth. She was just like the wee lassies back on the mainland.

---

[4]*ron*—seal (Gaelic)

After ten days had passed I began to get a feeling in my fingers, they began to feel better which shouldn't have been for weeks! But she still kept giving me these cups of evil-tasting medicine, like seaweed. After a few more days I began to rally and come to myself again. I promised to take her back to the mainland in the ship and introduce her to my wife and my sons. I loved her like my own daughter because I didn't have any daughters, I just had two sons. So I sat and told her cracks and tales and stories, I told her about Flippy the seal and how Flippy and I had spent such times together, how vexed I was when Flippy went and left me, how lonely it is for an old man like me to spend three months on a rock out in the sea with nobody to speak to for days on end. And we became great friends. She did everything, I had nothing to do. I felt perfect except for this damned arm, but it got better every day.

Then one morning the sun shone bright and clearly. I was lying in my bed. Rona used to always come in and give me a cup of tea every morning and waken me up because she slept in another wee room in a cubby hole in the cupboard where I made a bed for her. But I waited and waited, waited and waited for my morning cuppy, which I had got accustomed to. It never came. I managed to get up on my own, and this time my arm felt a bit better. And I knew that within a week the boat would relieve me, I would be back home to my wife. I could see my own doctor, get it fixed perfectly. I waited and I called around the lighthouse, around the rooms. There was not a sight of her to be seen. I searched every place I could find but Rona was gone.

I went back to my bedroom and I sat, I worried. I had no time for tea, nothing. I was so vexed and so sad I didn't know what to do. I had no time for breakfast, I was so sad. I said, "Prob'ly she went out swimmin and she got drowned." And I was so upset, I didn't know what to do. I searched the island, I went down the steps, searched the lighthouse outside and inside. She was gone, there was no Rona.

I came back up the steps and said, "I wonder where in the world that wee lassie has gone." And I walked into my bedroom, to the bed right there where I slept. And what do you think was staring me right in the face? Now you're not going to believe this, but the room was empty, the lighthouse was empty, and Rona was gone. But there were three slippers left in a row in front of my bed. Three slippers—left in a row in front of my bed! I knew then that Flippy had come back to help me for helping her, for she was a silkie! And that's the end of my story.

———

Away back in the West Coast a long time ago, there once lived a lighthouse keeper. He lived on the mainland and he had a wife and two children. But every four months he used to go out to this lighthouse on a rock off the coast. And the keeper was in that lighthouse on the rock for three months at a time. It was a hard time to be a lighthouse keeper in these days because the pay was poor and you were cut off from everybody; you never saw your relations, you were very lucky if a boat ever came to you. Now this old keeper's name was Peter MacKinnon. He came back to the mainland for a month after his time was served on the rock; he called it "The Rock."

One night I was lucky to meet Peter in a pub. He was a wee bit upset as he sat in the bar-room of this wee pub. And I could see by the way he told this story to us—we were sitting round the table listening—that he really believed it. I don't know if you believed the story or not, I don't know what you feel about it, but this was the way Peter told "Lighthouse Keeper" to me. I can remember, I was so taken away with that story . . . You see, silkies didn't make themselves known, say, "I'm a silkie, you must believe me, I'm a great silkie!" They came as a coincidence

to people who really needed them at the time. That's what
makes silkie stories so good ... they're here and they're
gone. It's only certain people in the world who have had the
experience.

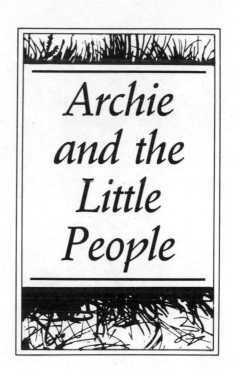

Archie
and the
Little
People

any years ago, long before your day and mine, as my granny used to say, away in a wee croft in the West Highlands, there lived an old crofter and his wife. They kept some sheep and some goats. And they had a daughter and a son. But the father really loved the son from his heart because he was the youngest. Wherever he went, he took his son with him. By taking his son with him every place he went, even to the sheep markets and to the cattle markets, the daughter left behind became very jealous of her wee brother. She loved her daddy very much.

But time has a habit of passing by, and it wasn't very long before the mother died and the father died. The croft was left to the son and daughter. She was a bit older than her brother, so she maintained that she was the boss, she was the owner. And she came down upon her young brother—there was nothing in the world that he could do was right! He did his work, took care of the sheep, took care of the farm, milked the cow, looked after the goats and everything else. But whenever he came back near teatime, she flung his supper on the table and said, "There's yir supper!" He and his sister could never be good friends. She never gave him any peace. His name was Archie.

But time passed by and Archie got used to this. His sister domineered him in every way—"Do this; do that; Archie, do this; Archie, do that; Archie, take yir boots aff; Archie, get sticks; Archie, bring in the water!" And poor Archie did everything that his sister told him because she was a few years older than he. But he still had to go out in the hills to take care of his sheep.

And the years passed by; Archie grew up till he came about the age of twenty-five. Still his sister domineered him in every way. He had his bed up the stairs, and some nights he was quite glad to crawl in to get away from her. She never gave him a good word. She treated him like dirt. In her own mind she was jealous because she'd loved her father very much and he had never shown her any affection. Now her father and mother were gone she took it out on Archie. She couldn't think of bad enough things to do on him. And Archie took it all with good heart; he was a kindly soul and never gave it much thought. Every morning she filled a wee bottle of milk for him and gave him a *piece*[1] and said, "There's yir piece, there's yir bag, and get out tae the hill and take care o' yir sheep!" And this went on for years. He had two wee beautiful collie dogs and she hated them too. Nothing in the world that Archie could do seemed to please her. She wouldn't let him drink, wouldn't let him smoke; she wouldn't let him do anything, and he was glad to escape up the stairs to his bed at night-time. They were like enemies.

Then one morning, it was the first of May. She came down the stairs from her bedroom. She said to Archie, "Yir breakfast is ready! Get yir breakfast and get out tae the hill and take care o' the sheep!"

Poor Archie never said a word.

"Yir milk is ready, yir piece is ready, yir dogs are fed!" This is the way she went on. And poor Archie *was* upset this morning—they never had a kindly word for each other.

So that morning, the first day in May, Archie picked up his bottle of milk and his little sandwich that his sister had made for him, called on his two dogs, and went out on the hill to take care of his sheep. He wandered through the hillside for a

---

[1]*piece*—sandwich

long long while, whistling to see if any sheep *was cowped*[2] on
its back or any one had maggots on its back or any one was
hurt; he herded all the sheep for the full half day. Then the
sun was high—it was about twelve o'clock. He came to this
large rock which he had passed by many's a time but never
had stopped at. Then he thought to himself that the sun was
so hot he would find the shade of the rock on one side, sit
down there and have his bottle of milk and his piece, in peace
and quiet.

He called the two dogs beside him and opened his little bag,
shared his lunch with the dogs, and drank his bottle of milk.
But all in a moment, all in a moment he was surrounded by
all these little people! And the dogs gave a bark and cleared
out! Archie wondered why the dogs should run away. But
sure enough, before you could say another word, he was
surrounded by these little people. And he was sitting with his
back against the rock, his legs stretched out, his bottle down
beside him and his wee bag for holding his piece and his
scissors—the shears for clipping the sheep—on the other side.
They came round in dozens, they climbed on his knee, they
climbed on his back, up, and they pulled his hair, they checked
his ears, looked into them. And Archie was so amazed.

Then all in a moment, up came one who was a little bigger
than the rest. He said, "Stop! Leave him alone. Come down
here and behave yourselves!"

Archie looked up. There before him stood the most beautiful little man he'd ever seen in his life, with a beautiful crown
on his head. The sun was shining on it. It was sparkling as if
it were made of diamonds, sparkling like diamonds.

He said, "Hello, Archie!"

Archie rubbed his eyes, he thought he was asleep. He said,
"Hello!"

And when the King spoke, every little one gathered behind
him and went down on their knees. And the King stood

---

[2]*was cowped*—had fallen over

before Archie. "Archie, I'm sorry. You'll hev tae move away from here."

And Archie said, "Why should I move away from here?"

"Well," he said, "you can move or you don't need to, because we are gaunnae have a party here."

And Archie said, "Who are youse?"

He said, "Archie, you ought to know who we are!"

"Well," he said, "I don't really know . . . and I'm trying tae believe it but I canna believe it!"

He said, "Archie, we are the Little People, we're the fairies! This is the day we're gaunnae have wir party here!"

Archie says, "Please don't send me away. You know I'm lonely."

"We know," says the little man, says the King of the Fairies, "we know how you're tortured with your sister and how she rules yir life! You have never had nothing." And he turned round and spoke to some of them in a kind of foreign language that Archie couldn't understand.

Then up comes a little man with a wee barrel and he pulls off the lid. He hands it to Archie and Archie looks, he smells it.

"Drink it!" says the King. "Drink it up!"

And Archie drank it up. And he felt this beautiful warmness crawling down through his body and he felt so light, he felt so gay. He turned to the King and said, "I have never enjoyed anything like that before in my life. Have you any more?"

"Oh, ye like it?" said the King.

Archie said, "I like it—I love it!"

The King pointed his finger; another wee man came up with another one and pulled off the lid. Archie drank it. And then another one was brought and Archie drank it.

"Now," said the King, "I see you enjoy our way and our drink."

Archie said, "I never enjoyed nothing like this before in my life." Then *gone* was the thought of his sister, *gone* was the thought of his dogs, *gone* was the thought of everything! This

was all he wanted to see. He said, "Come up, little one!" And
he took hold of one of them. And they climbed up and sat on
his knees. Then Archie began to diddle the mouth music. He
was a good diddler and all the little ones began to dance.
Archie went,

And the King said, "Ye're good," and they all clapped their
hands!
And Archie felt happy as he'd never felt before in his life.
All the Little People were shouting, "More, more, more!",
clapping their hands, "give us more, give us more!"

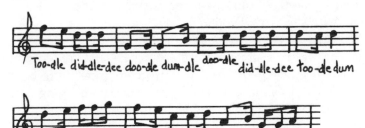

And they started to dance again. The King said, "Please, please, Archie . . . we told you a little while ago tae leave, but don't leave now!"

And Archie's sitting with his feet stretched out and his back against the rock. Now he's in good company, the finest company he's ever had in his life. He indulged in the Little People's drink and had their company. He wanted nothing else in the world.

The King snapped his fingers once more and they came up with another barrel; Archie drank it. And then he diddled, he diddled and danced, diddled and danced. The sun rose higher in the sky—one o'clock. The sun moved on.

Now back home his old sister's worried because it's six o'clock in the night. To Archie it only seemed five minutes, as if he had only sat five minutes.

Then the King came up and said to Archie, "Archie, that is beautiful. But I'll tell ye something, yir sister is getting worried and we don't want ye tae get intae trouble."

So Archie stood up and staggered a wee bit, picked up his bag, and said to the Little People, "I'll be back!"

And the Fairy King said to him, "Well, ye better make it soon because it's a long time till May-month next year!"

Archie walked back across the moor, and by the time he landed back, it was seven o'clock in the evening. He knew in his heart that the Little People had another five hours to go. He said to himself, "Five hours till twelve o'clock. Is it me gaunna spend five hours with that sister o' mine, or is it five hours with the Little People?"

So when he landed back at his little farm where his sister lived, he was in a great state of happiness and contentment. He walked in the door. And the two dogs were lying on the floor, their eyes shining in the light, their ears hanging down. They hid under the table when they saw Archie coming.

And the sister stepped to the door. "Where have you been?"

He said, "I have been with my friends, what do you think?"

Archie felt no fear of her anymore. To him she was like somebody he'd never known!

She said, "Where have you been? Do you know what time it is?"

"Of course," he said, "I know what time it is. It's about seven o'clock."

"Where have you been? Have you been drinking?"

"Of course I've been drinking!"

"I've warned all these friends o' yours not to give you nae drink!"

He said, "The friends that gave me the drink are the dearest friends of all tae me!" And he says, "See you, old crow! I can drink and I can sing, and I can diddle!"

She says, "Come and get yir supper! Yir dogs have come home and made me worried."

He says, "Keep yir dogs and keep yir supper because I want nothing from you anymore! I have seen the light of the world, I have been among the Little People."

She says, "The Little People! I know it's them that did it tae you. They've done this to you, you've met the Little People. And rue be upon ye!"

He says, "Rue be upon you! Keep yir supper, keep yir dogs, keep yir food, keep yir farm! I have four hours till twelve o'clock." And he turned round. He walked out the door and banged it behind him. He was gone.

And he travelled back to the hill once more, joined the Little Folk. He diddled and he danced and sang till twelve o'clock. But when the second of May came, Archie was gone. She waited and she waited and she waited for evermore. But Archie was never seen again. And that is the end of my story.

The
Broonie's
Curse

Many many years ago, long before your time and mine, away in the back highlands of Argyllshire in a wee village, there once lived this hotel keeper and he had this big hotel. And he used to cater for the tourists in the summertime who came for hunting and shooting, and spent their summer holidays in the hotel. When he catered for fifteen or twenty people the hotel was full. And while the hotel was full, he had little time for other people around the village whom he depended on in the wintertime. The villagers didn't think much of him, he wasn't liked very much.

Now the hotel was situated on the banks of a fresh water loch. And from this loch there ran a river into the sea, and on the other side, about a hundred yards across the river, was a valley. In this wee valley were a lot of houses and crofts. And the hotel man used to employ an old man called Donald. He and his old wife had a wee croft, and he used to take a rowing boat, row the people across to the hotel when they needed a dram or when they needed to go for any messages, because the hotel was a post office and a shop.

But anyway, it was about the month of June and the summer tourist season was at its peak; all the tourists were gathered in the hotel, it was full up! It was evening, about five or six o'clock, and so warm that everyone had taken their drinks out into the garden. They were all sitting round the tables talking and speaking to each other, when down the path from the main road that led into the garden walked an old

91

tramp man, with a wee white beard and a long tattered coat, dusty but clean.

The hotel owner was sitting discussing the weather with some of the tourists at a table. The old man walked straight up—how he knew, I don't know—but he walked up to the hotel owner, stood before him. And the owner stood up. "What do you want, old man?"

The old man said, "I'm lookin fir work, have ye any kind o' work I cuid do?"

And the hotel owner looked at him. "*You* lookin fir work, in here, in this place?"

The old man said, "Yes, I'm luikin fir work. I'll do any kind o' work you have, dig your garden, anything you want."

The hotel owner said, "We don't need tramps tae do any work, we have people who do these things. And remember auld man . . . *be* on your way! We've no work here fir ye."

The old man stood. "Well, if I canna help you, could you help me?"

"What kind o' help do you want?" the hotel owner said.

He said, "Cuid you give me something to eat? I'm very hungry."

And the hotel owner said, "Well, there's a couple o' bins round the back where the cook throws out some bones; if you walk round you might get some bones in the bin. But you better hurry before the dogs get them. And, old man, if I wis you I wad be on my way shortly, because we'll soon be closin up. I'll be lettin the dogs loose in a moment. I hope they don't catch ye on the grounds o' the hotel when night falls."

And all the tourists laughed at the hotel owner making a fool of the old tramp man.

The old tramp man walked out the gate muttering to himself and down the wee path—he knew where he was going, how he knew only he could tell! He walked out muttering and the people all laughed at him. He walked down the wee path that led to the shoreside. About twenty yards from the front of the hotel was the loch, and this narrow path with some steps led down to the waterside where the boatman took people across to the other side where all the crofts and farms were.

Now the boatman, Donald, by this time was just after coming across to see if anybody was needing to go out fishing, because that's what he was employed for, to take the gentry out on this wee loch to fish. Now it was only a penny to cross the loch because it wasn't very far, a hundred yards to the other side. As Donald was pulling in the boat and tying it up where the people wouldn't get their feet wet, who came walking down the steps but the old tramp man. Donald turned round when he saw the old man coming, he stood and looked and heard him muttering away to himself—what he was saying nobody knows.

So Donald, being a kind-hearted soul, said, "Hello, auld man, are ye wantin across the loch tae the other side?"

He said, "Yes, I want across, the're not very much fir me here."

And when Donald looked he saw an old man with a ragged coat, ragged but clean; an old tramp with his wee gray beard and the two most beautiful blue eyes he'd ever seen in his life looking straight at Donald. Donald couldn't even look at his eyes. He said, "You want me tae take you across the river?"

"Yes," he said, "I want you tae take me across the river, I might find some work on the other side."

And Donald said, "Where did you come from?"

"I came down frae the hotel. I was up there and I asked fir work. I'm very hungry and very poor. And," he said, "they laughed at me, made a fool of me. So would you take me across tae the other side?"

Donald said, "It's a penny tae take ye across. One penny. But seein ye're an auld tramp, I'll take ye across fir nothing. In fact, there's nobody gaun fishin, so I'll take ye across right noo."

So Donald jumped in the boat and the old man jumped in and sat down in the back. Donald rowed him across to the other side of the loch, pulled up the boat. After they'd crossed, Donald stepped out first to pull his boat up, and then the old tramp stepped out.

The old tramp said, "Thank you." And he put his hand in his pocket, took out a coin, and handed it to Donald. "That'll pay fir takin me across." And Donald never even looked at it, he put it in his pocket, thought it was a penny.

"Auld tramp," he said, "there wadnae be much doon at the hotel right noo. If ye're hungry, come on up and meet my wife, she'll prob'ly give ye something tae eat."

"Thank you," said the old tramp. "I wad really like that very much."

So the old man and Donald walked, about ten or twelve yards from the wee place where they docked the boat, up to Donald's croft, a wee house and a couple of buildings. They walked up the wee path through a wee field. On the croft Donald kept some goats and a cow and couple of calves. But meantime he spent his time in the water, rowing the boat for tourists for the fishing.

Donald said, "Come in."

The old man said, "No, it's no my policy tae walk intae other people's hooses. I cuidna go, I don't go into people's hooses."

So Donald walked in, his wife said, "Ye're back early, Donald."

"Well, I had a funny experience," he said.

She said, "What happened?"

"Well," he said, "I rowed over across tae the hotel and I wis jist tyin up the boat when an old man, an old tramp man—who I think is a tramp—cam walkin doon the path. And there's something queer about him, something I don't understand. And I took him across tae this side, he was luikin fir work, he seemed so terrible insultit by the hotel owner."

"Donald, ye know what kind o' man the hotel owner is—he wad insult anybody," she said, "even yirsel sometimes. What's yir problem?"

"Well," he said, "he's hungry, I think he's hungry."

"Well," she said, "I'll give him a bowl o' soup, tell him tae come in."

He said, "I've asked him in, I've asked him but he wadnae come."

"If he'll no come in," the woman said, "I'll take a bowl o' soup oot tae him."

So the old woman filled a big clay bowl full of soup and put in a wooden spoon, and went out. The old tramp was sitting on the steps of the door. She gave the old man the bowl of soup with the wooden spoon, and when the old tramp looked at the spoon his eyes lighted up. She looked into his eyes, she was aghast when she saw these beautiful blue eyes—the way he looked at her when he saw the wooden spoon in the bowl.

She said, "Auld man, my husband says ye're hungry."

"Yes, my dear, I'm hungry."

"Well," she said, "would ye accept this bowl o' soup?"

He said, "I wad love a bowl o' soup." She gave the old tramp the soup and he supped it with the wooden spoon. After he was finished he handed the bowl back and thanked Donald's wife very much.

And he said, "I'll go away up now, I'll see if I can find any work up among the crofts on the hillside." The old man walked away.

When she came back in Donald was sitting down in the kitchen. "Donald, I had the queerest experience."

"Did you feel that too," he said to her, "did you feel that too?"

"Donald, that's no a tramp," she said, "no way."

He said, "Did you think that too?"

"That's no tramp," she said, "did you see his eyes?"

"Of course," he said, "I saw his eyes."

"He hes the bluest eyes I ever saw in my life," she said, "and as bright as a bird! But not only that, ye never saw his eyes when he saw my wooden spoon."

"There's something queer about it, I don't know . . . but tramp or no tramp," Donald says, "he managed tae pay his way across the ferry."

She says, "Donald, you shouldn't have taken it. It's prob'ly the last penny the poor cratur had. Give it tae me, and I'll run efter him and give it back tae him!"

Donald put his hand in his pocket—now he didn't have any money of any description, he never carried money with him—hand in his pocket and brought out the coin. He looked at it . . . a five-pound gold piece! (And you believe me, in these days five pounds was a terrible lot of money, a man would work a year for five pounds!) Donald had put the gold piece in his pocket as a coin.

"Luik," he says, "there's what he gave me."

She says, "Donald, that was no tramp. There's queer things will happen before this night's oot!"

They looked out the door in the distance. It was a good bit from Donald's croft up to the next crofts, but the road was empty. Then *all fared well.*[1] But they talked about it all night and didn't rest very well.

The next morning, as usual after breakfast, Donald got in his boat, rowed across to the hotel about eight o'clock. He tied his boat up, walked up to the hotel, everything was quiet and peaceful. There wasn't a soul to be seen.

"Och," he said to himself, "I wonder what's the problem this morning. Mebbe everybody had a hard night last night and everybody is asleep." He walked up to the hotel, knocked on the door. The hotel owner came out but he was hardly able to stand.

Donald said, "Good morning, sir, are any customers goin fishin this morning?"

---

[1]*all fared well*—nothing else happened

"Och," he said, "there's nobody fir ye this morning, and there's nobody fir ye tomorrow morning: everybody is down with the sickness."

Donald said, "Whit?"

"Down with the sickness," he said, "every guest I've got is sick in bed. And we've sent fir the doctor, he canna find what's wrong wi them."

"That's queer," Donald said, "that's a queer-queer thing. What did the doctor say about it?"

"The doctor said it's confined here. It's in the food, the food's contaminated, or mebbe the water. All my visitors is completely sick in the hotel, not able. So," he said, "Donald, I don't think there's very much ye can do this morning."

"That's queer," he said. "Is there anybody in the village, the people that was in the hotel drinkin . . ."

"No," he said, "it seems that the people in the village is all right." And the hotel owner was completely upset.

So there wasn't much Donald could do. "Sir, if the're nothing fir me to dae, the're nobody to take oot tae fish this morning," he said, "I'll prob'ly go back and find a job in the croft tae mysel."

So Donald goes back down, turns his boat and rows across the loch, ties his boat up. His wife is surprised to see him back.

She says, "Donald, what's the matter, is there no fishin today? How about yir guests?"

"Och, guests," he says. "Aye, there's no guests this morning, everyone in the hotel is completely sick, with the sickness."

She says, "What kind o' sickness?"

"Well," he says, "that's what the hotel owner told me. There's not one person cam oot o' the hotel this morning wi the sickness, there's nobody can move."

"I knew it!" she says. "I knew it! The minute I saw that old tramp man comin up yesterday and your five-pound gold

piece—Donald, you believe me—that was no tramp, that was
the Broonie! That was the Broonie and that is his curse on
him fir what he did, it'll prob'ly learn him a lesson fir what he
did on the Broonie. But wait—you'll see, Donald," she says,
"mark my words: the worst is yet tae come!"

"Ach away, wumman," he says, "the Broonie! That's only
a story, only a story."

She says, "Donald, story or no story . . . but you believe
me, the worst is tae come. That's only the beginnin."

So anyway, all that day Donald worked about his croft, did
his own jobs. But next morning he rowed his boat across once
more to the hotel. And sure enough, when he landed at the
hotel the hotel owner had got up, but he was the only one
able. The rest of them were all in bed with the sickness. And
the local doctor was there. Donald was lucky to meet him
coming out from the hotel just as he was going up the steps to
see if anybody was wanting to go fishing with the hot weather.
The doctor and Donald were well known to each other.

"Oh good morning, Donald," he said.

"Oh good morning, Doctor," he said. "What's the problem?"

"Well, Donald," he said, "tae tell ye the truth, I don't
know mysel what's the problem. These people are sufferin
from a sickness and I cannae find what's wrong wi them.
They cannae eat or cannae sleep, in no way. They're no
ill—but they're sick."

And Donald said, "Is there anybody in the village sufferin
fae the same complaint?"

"No way at all," he said, "there's not one complaint in the
village."

Donald said, "Is it contagious, will it spread?"

"Luik, as far as I know," the doctor said, "it'll not spread
nae farther than the hotel, because there were people drinkin
in the hotel and they walked home . . . they're just as safe as
anybody. It's confined to the hotel."

So Donald bade the doctor good-bye, and the doctor went

away about his business. Donald took his boat, rowed back to his wife, and told her the whole story.

"I knew it, Donald," she said, "I knew it. I knew that's the trouble—it's a curse. There's nobody in their right mind would tell the Broonie tae go and get a bone oot o' the bin."

"But how was the man tae know that he was the Broonie—if you call it the Broonie—how was the man tae know?" he said. "I know that nobody likes the hotel owner, apart fae mycel, but the man's a man and my employment depends on him. And why should the Broonie put a curse on the people?"

"Well, Donald," she said, "you don't understand. It's not exactly a curse, it's just a way o' tellin the man tae be kinder to all the other sowls like himsel, wha comes aboot the doors."

For seven days the sickness raged in the hotel. And nobody was allowed near the place. Nobody could eat, nobody could sleep. But after seven days had passed everybody was right as rain. And the tourists were glad to be free of the hotel. Everyone, the sportsmen, the shooters, the fishers, all packed up and went home, on their way. But the word spread round about the hotel that was contaminated with the sickness, and for the whole fearin summer not one single soul of a tourist ever came near it. And the hotel owner had to depend on the local people for survival. People that he hated and people who didn't like him came to his hotel. That's all he had. And he sat and discussed the situation with them, and by discussing with the local people he came to know the villagers who came across in Donald's boat to the hotel for a drink. And by coming to know these people he gained a better understanding. But Donald never brought up the subject to the hotel owner about the old tramp man.

And from that day on till the day the hotel owner died, never again did he ever turn an old tramp man or anybody looking for work, away from his door. And that's the last of my story.

This story was told to me many years ago when I was young by an old cousin of my mother's, an old man called Sandy Townsley. I travelled through Aberdeenshire with him and his family. We didn't have any ponies or any motor cars, just a wee handcart, we packed our tents on it. So after walking all day, and his old woman hawking the houses all day from door to door, we got kind of tired and we put up the bow tents in this wee woodside. The old woman went to her bed, the children went to theirs, and he and I kindled this big fire in front of the tents. I wasn't very old, about seventeen or eighteen. So we're sitting telling cracks and newsin to each other.

"Brother," Sandy said to me, "you go for a kettle o' water." And I went over to a shed beside an old mill and a couple of knocked-down buildings, a wee burn coming down from the hill fell into this old mill wheel. I went round the back of the wheel and where the stream came down I filled the kettle. I came back to our camping place, which was covered in broom. Old Sandy said, "Did ye get the water?"

I said, "Aye, I got the water."

"Well," he said, "make a wee cup o' tea."

"Tae tell you something, Sandy," I said, "I bet you a pound the Broonie's in that mill ower there."

"Ho," he said, "dinna speak! The Broonie is everywhere. But if he's ony place, he'll be there."

I said, "Will he bide there?"

"No, the Broonie disna bide there, the Broonie on'y comes tae certain places. And he comes tae certain kinds o' folk!"

I said, "What kind o' folk does he come tae?"

"Ah," he said, "he disna come to every kind of folk, but he comes especially tae bad folk."

I said, "Have you got any good stories how he cam tae bad folk?"

"*Well,*" *he said, "I remember a story at wis tellt tae me by me faither a long time ago way back in Argyllshire.*"

I said, "'Tell it tae me, Uncle!"

"*Well,*" *he said, "brother, I'll tell ye a wee story.*" *And this is the story he told me.*

You don't "live happily ever after" with the Broonie, because he goes on his way. He's taught the people their lesson—that's the way the Broonie works. Now the Broonie's going to turn up again some other place . . .

The Fisherman and His Sons

here once lived this crofter in Argyll and his was a large croft on the coast with a good wee bit of land. And the old man had done a bit of fishing when his children were small. Now he had five sons all together, and when they grew up there wasn't enough work on the croft to keep the five of them plus the father, who was getting a wee bit up in years and tired of fishing. So they sat down at the table one evening and discussed their future.

The young lads said, "Well, Father, there's not much work for us all here between the croft and the fishin."

One lad said, "We'll hev tae try and work out an agreement or we'll hev tae move out and find employment somewhere else."

Now the old man didn't want his sons to go away and leave him because it was a large house, they had a good boat, and they had some cattle, some sheep, and a couple of horses. So this one evening while the five lads and their mother sat at the table, he said, "Well, sons, I've thought it over. Now I'm gettin kind o' up in years, the best thing I cuid do is turn the boat over to youse three young ones and let yese make a kirk or a mill of it!" (Meaning "win or lose," see!) "Me and yir two brothers, I think we cuid manage tae run the croft between hus. Whatever youse make from the sea is yir own . . . mebbe help out yir mother with a few pound for yir keep." Because fishing in these days was really good.

So they made an agreement, the two oldest brothers would work on the croft with their father and the three youngest ones would take over the boat and the nets, work on the sea. The three young lads were to do nothing on the croft, the father and the two oldest sons were to do nothing on the shore.

Everything fared well. Now they stayed at the side of this sea loch and it could be pretty rough water sometimes. But across from where they stayed, maybe two miles out, there was an island. And this was a good wee lump of island. There was no habitation on it but it was a home for the seals, hundreds of them.

The old man, when his family was young, used to sail round the island, fish round it, set his nets. Sometimes when he came out and pulled up his nets, maybe a fish was halved through the middle, a big cod was eaten by a seal. He would just catch it, throw it back in the water. "Ach well," he would say to himself, "the poor creatures needs a bite like mysel." He never complained about one single thing to his old woman. Life went on like that till he finally gave up the boat to the three lads.

Now the three young men took over the fishing, set their nets, had a good fishing, sent their fish into the market. There was a village and a pier not far away where people sold their fish. Because along the whole West Coast in these days every little village had fishing boats, some had big boats, some only had sailing boats without engines. And they all had the posts up along the shore for drying nets. So the three young men did pretty well for the first two or three months. But then it started—the seals began to start on their fish—holes in their nets, good fish eaten in half, some with only tails and heads stuck in the net where the seals had eaten them. So every time they came back home at night-time to their father (they all stayed in the one big house, there were none of them married) and sat down to their supper, they would start to complain.

"Well, boys," the father would say, "how did youse get on today, how did the fishin go?"

"Ach, not too good, Father," his son said, "not too good. The problem is thae seals—if it wasnae for the seals we could make a good livin."

The father said, "Boys, I've worked these shores long before youse were born and efter when youse were on'y children. And I managed to rear youse up to young men to take care of yirsels. I got my share of the fish, and the share that I didna get, the seals got. *They* have families, you know, they have tae feed their young too, as well as you. And the best thing you could do is leave these people alone." The old man called them "people."

"Father," the son said, "it might be all right with you in yir time, but now times are different, times are changin. You are all right on the land, you and wir brothers, wir two older brothers is makin a livin. But we've tae depend on the sea for wir livelihood, and if it wasnae for these seals we could do better."

Father said, "Luik, boys, I'm gaunna tell youse once and tell yese only wonst: I don't want youse comin back here every night and complainin tae me about the seals! Because the seals are my friends and always will be. Take what ye can get and be thankful. Stop complainin about the seals or if ye do—I'm only tellin ye—it could be worse for yirsels."

The young men never paid any attention to their father. "Ach, he's gettin auld," they talked among themselves, "he disna understand, he's quite happy wi the croft and our brothers." But they carried on fishing; some days they had were good, some days were bad, some days their nets weren't touched, some days their nets were cut where the seals went right through them. Some days the fish were destroyed, good fish in the nets. This began to get the young men down. They never complained to their father any more, but they complained among themselves.

They used to sail round the island, and they saw, about six or seven o'clock in the evening, that the seals would all come out on the rocks and hobble into this wee bay, hundreds of them. On the face of the island were steep cliffs where the gulls used to nest; the boys had gathered eggs here when they were young. But a small bay went into the island, a cove where all the driftwood had piled up and the grass grew close to the rocks. You couldn't go any further into the island unless you climbed the rocks, a hundred and fifty feet up the cliff face. There was only one way into this bay, from the sea; there was no way you could come in from the land. It was sheltered and this is where the seals used to come, lie and bask in the evening.

So one evening the three young men came in early from the fishing. They made up a plan that they would take clubs, go and kill all the young seals they could find and stone the big seals to death, try and rid the island of them. They never spoke a word to their father but just walked out, said they were going to check on their boat. The two older brothers, sitting by the fireside after working hard all day on their wee bit of land, never paid any attention. They were reading books, maybe the Bible, or reading the paper. The old mother was baking and the old father was lying back in his chair, maybe half asleep.

The three young men slipped away. Quietly they took their boat, rowed out to the island with their clubs. They went round the island first, then rowed into the small cove. When they landed there wasn't a seal to be seen, not one.

"Brother," one said, "it's queer, it's queer. The're always plenty o' them."

After rowing about two miles to the island, they weren't going to row back straightaway, see! They said, "We'll wait," and one said, "They're bound tae come in on the rocks sometime this evening because they always do!" Even after the sun set, after they'd been eating all day, they came up to rest on the rocks. Young seals, half-grown seals, baby seals, old seals, all kinds climbed up on to the top of the rocks. Some swam into the bay and climbed up on this wee grassy cove.

This cove is where the boys had pulled up their boat. So

they walked in on the grass, they cracked and talked for a wee while about what they were going to do. "Well," says one of the brothers, "if we're gaunna wait, we'll have a small fire. We could sit here till the seals comes up the rocks. Then we'll knock hell out o' them wi stones, stone them tae death. And the ones that we can reach we'll kill wi wir clubs!"

So that they wouldn't be seen, they went further into this wee cove to a sheltered corner where all the driftwood had piled up. They kindled a small fire and sat down. They were talking and smoking, waiting for the seals. They waited maybe an hour.

The youngest said, "Shst, listen! Listen! I hear something."

"Oh," one said, "it's prob'ly the seals comin in."

"No," he said, "it's no seals—it's voices."

"Voices?" the other said. "There's nobody here, nobody here, the're nae voices here. It canna be people because the're no people, very seldom people."

But they heard voices coming closer. Voices were coming closer—then all in a moment they were surrounded by a colony of folk. There must have been a hundred and fifty, all came in behind them. Now there was no escape except up the cliff face.

The three young men sat with a wee fire and they looked, they didn't know what to do. They were aghast. They'd never seen people like this before—dressed in furry kind of suits. And they were talking among themselves, some talking in half Gaelic, half broken English and Gaelic. Now the boys themselves had good Gaelic and could understand some of what they were saying. There were voices said, "That's them, they're the ones."

The three young men stood up—they didn't know what to do because there were too many of them. There were young ones, young boys, young lassies, bairns, wee toddlers, old women and old men! A hundred and fifty folk surrounded these young men. There's no escape, no way!

This big one, the biggest of the lot, walked forward. The

boys could see he was gray in the hair and dressed in these droll kind of furry clothes, the likes of which the boys had never seen in their lives before. They were terrified! They were only young men in their teens, you know! They didn't know what to do.

And this big one stepped forward. I'll say what he said but I can't say it the way he said it. "Well, young men," he said in broken English and Gaelic mixed, "yese came here tonight on a purpose."

They couldn't speak—were dumbfounded.

And he said, "Your purpose was here—fir tae come and stone the seals tae death—*hus*, stone hus! Kill wir children and destroy wir babies."

And the oldest of the three brothers said, "Sir . . . but youse are not seals. We have never interfered with you . . . where do youse come from? We've never seen youse before, how can you condemn hus fir destroyin the seals which his got nothing tae do wi you?"

And this man said, "You have come here to stone the seals—*we* are the seal-folk and you hev come here tae destroy hus. Ye meant . . . everything ye intend tae do is upon hus. So we cam here tonight tae do the same thing tae you."

The seal-folk all gathered round each other. They mumbled and they talked, mumbled and talked among each other. Now these three young men are terrified!

The older folk gathered round and had this meeting. Finally they said, "We've held court and we're gaunnae stone youse tae death, do the same thing, what you were gaunnae do to us. You've been condemned to death, the same you promised hus—there's no escape fir ye."

The young men didn't know what to do. They tried to make excuses but it was no good.

Then all in a minute, behind them came hobbling up, with a piece of driftwood under one arm, an old old man with a long white beard, dressed in the same kind of furs, droll kind of skin. "Stop, stop, stop!" he said in Gaelic. And the boys knew what he was saying.

The spokesman, the biggest man with the gray hair, said, "What is it, Grandfather?"

"Stop!" he said. "Wait!" The old man came up to the front, stood before the young men. "Young men, ye know what you've come here tae do tonight. Ye came here tae destroy hus seal-folk, hus people, and stone hus tae death. Well, prob'ly you wouldn't have stoned us all tae death, you cuid hev hurt some of wir children or destroyed some of wir babies. But my son here wants me to reap revenge upon you. Now," he said, "yir father warned you many many times to leave hus people alone! *We* take some fish from yir nets because they're floatin in the water, we take them from the net because there's many many more in other places to catch, apart from around here. What is round this island we say is ours."

The three young men were too flabbergasted to speak, they couldn't talk back for themselves.

"But," he said, "I'm gaunnae let you go this time with a warnin. Remember what I tell ye." So he turns round to all the other folk and says to this oldest son of his, "Listen, son, I want ye tae let these young men go."

"But, Father," he says, "ye know what they hev come to do!"

"Son," he said, "remember one thing: if it wasn't for this young men's father, *you* or me wouldn't be here today—that's why I want tae give them a chance. I never tellt ye this before, but I'm gaunnae tell ye now."

"Well," the son said, "you'd better make it good!"

"I'll tell ye," he said. "Many many years ago when I was a young seal, I wis tangled in that children's father's net and rope—I went in fir a fish and I was caught. He pulled me up and he set me free. Now," he says, "I want you tae set these young men free. Now," he says, "remember, young men, we are the seal-folk: you leave hus alone and we'll leave you alone!"

So they stepped back one and all. And the three young men ran to their boat and jumped in. They rowed as fast as they could. When they came back that night and beached their boat, walked into their father's house, they were as white as ghosts.

The father looked, and they could hardly speak. The father said, "Well, sons, where have yese been?"

"Oh, Father," one said, "we were out on the island, on Seal Island, there for a while looking around to see if . . . tae find a good fishin spot."

"And, boys, did ye find a good spot that wad suit youse?"

"No, Father," he said, "I don't think so. We didnae find a good spot, it disna look very good, it looks kind o' rough. In fact, I think in the future we'll take yir word for it and keep away from Seal Island—leave the fish there," he said, "*fir your sea-folk.*" And that's the end of my story!

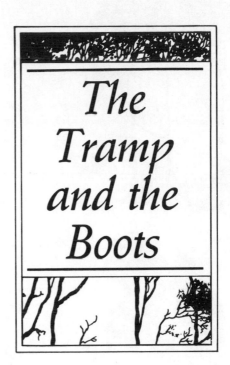

The
Tramp
and the
Boots

he old tramp was weary and tired, for he had walked all morning along the dusty highway, which in these days was just a track across the country. He had travelled for many days and come across very few places where he could find any food. All he'd had for the last two days was a rabbit he'd found by the roadside roasted over a fire.

He said to himself, "If I don't find some habitation, a farm or a croft or something along the highway before nightfall, I'm sure I'm going to be very hungry." Because these old tramps begged whatever they could, whatever they needed to eat. It was only by the kindliness of the local people along the way that these tramps managed to survive. And he'd travelled for so many miles his feet were sore . . . the day was hot and the sun was shining. It was a beautiful summer day. Even suppose he was so hungry, tiredness began to overcome the hunger.

And then he came down by this little hill. Beside the roadside he looked across the moor and *there* was the most beautiful little hill he'd ever seen, covered in daisies and flowers! He said to himself, "Wouldn't that be a nice place fir tae have a rest if I could afford tae rest." The hunger pains in his stomach were bothering him, but the soreness of his feet overcame them. He walked over to the little hill and he sat down.

He stretched himself out to rest and thought, "In such a lovely place, if a person wasna so hungry . . ."

He'd rested for a long while, three-quarters of an hour or

115

so, when all in a moment he heard a little voice saying, "Auld man, you'll hev to be gone from this place."

And the tramp looked around, saying to himself, "Am I hearin right? Is there someone talkin?" He looked all around, he could see nothing because the grass was high and the flowers were beautiful.

Then the voice spoke again, "Old man, you'll hev tae leave here."

And the tramp looked again . . . sure enough, there stood aside him a little man—not very big, maybe, say, twelve inches high, with a long white beard and a peakit cap and peakit shoes. The tramp was amazed because he had never seen anybody . . . he'd heard of people so small as that many many years before, but he'd never experienced meeting one. He couldn't hardly speak for a moment or two, he was so amazed.

Then he found his voice. "Little man," he said, "I am tired!"

And the little man said, "Old man, look, you must move from this place immediately!"

And the old tramp man said, "But who are you, little man? I have never seen anyone like you before."

The little man said, "Never mind who I am," and he came up closer to the old tramp man.

When he came a little closer, the old tramp man had to bend over and look down. The old tramp had pulled up his knees to himself and the little man hardly came as high as his knee . . . there he stood with his long white beard and his wee cap and curled shoes. And the tramp thought in his mind, "This is queer, this is very funny." He was so tired and weary, but with the excitement of seeing this little creature the hunger in his belly was forgotten about.

And the little man said, "Old man, you'll hev tae move."

The old tramp said, "Look, I am an auld tramp. I am weary. I have come a long long way and I am hungry. I have come here to rest." Now in these days a long time ago there were no fences along the way, no hedges; there were no roads. A person could walk off the track and sit down, rest theirself anywhere. So this is what the old tramp had done. He said to the little man, "Look, there's no reason why—that I can't rest here because this is a free place. I'm enjoyin myself on this little hill restin myself!"

And the little man said, "You must go!"

The tramp said, "Not tonight, I can't go another step!"

Then the little man saw he couldn't persuade him in any way. He said to the tramp, "What would you take to move on? Is it food you want?"

And the tramp said, "Not exactly food. My feet are sore, and food wouldn't make my feet any better."

The wee man looked down and saw the poor old tramp's boots were worn right through to the soles, with his toes sticking out. And the little man said, "I see yir feet really is in a sorry state."

"Yes," said the old tramp, "my feet are in a sorry state and they're really sore."

So the little man felt sorry for the tramp; he didn't argue or command him anymore. He asked, "Auld man, what would you really take to move from here?"

And the old tramp said, "Why is it so important I should move from here at this very moment?"

But the little man did not answer. "Well," he said, "what would you really take tae move from this hill?"

And the tramp said, "Well, I am hungry, the pains are botherin my stomach at this moment, and I wad like to go on to the next village or the next house or farm where I could find something to eat. But my feet are so sore and my boots are so worn . . . the pain overcomes my hunger."

So the little man said, "If you had a nice pair o' boots that made your feet comfortable, would you move on?"

The tramp said, "If I had some nice comfortable boots for my feet, I would surely be gone!"

The little man said, "Just wait a minute—I will find you some boots!"

Now the old tramp in his hunger thought he was dreaming. He thought he had fallen asleep. He looked around and the little man was gone, completely disappeared. He rubbed his eyes with his hands and thought, "I must have dozed over, I must hae been dreamin." And he looked around the little hill: all the flowers were blooming so beautifully. He thought to himself, "I'll jist spend the night here, relax and have a sleep." Because these old tramps always slept out in the open. They had no home or no place to go.

But he hadn't waited more than three to four minutes, when back comes the little man. And over his back he had a pair of boots. The tramp looked, saw the little man with the boots, and said, "I am not dreamin, I have not been asleep!"

And lo and behold, the little man came up beside his knee. But the boots were just small things. The little man said to the tramp, "I have brought you some boots and I hope you will keep to your promise."

But the tramp said, "Little man, I don't know where you came from, but do you realize that these boots would never fit my feet in any way—they wouldn't even fit my little toe!"

And the little man said, "Wait, jist wait and watch!" The little man looked at the tramp's feet, saw his old boots with holes in them and his toes sticking through. He measured the size that the old tramp's feet really were, and he placed the boots down on the ground. He waited.

And the tramp watched. The boots got bigger and bigger and bigger, till they came about the size that the tramp really needed, and then they stopped. The tramp looked—there before him were the most beautiful boots he had ever seen in his life. Many's the time the tramp had seen gentlemen and lairds and people of high degree with beautiful boots which he admired, but he had never owned a pair in his life. His one ambition in life was to own a beautiful pair of boots, because these tramps walked many many miles.

Then the tramp said, "I just can't believe it! Are these fir me?"

And the little man said, "Yes, they're for you! Old man, they're fir you! You can have them with good heart and good will," he said, "providin that you try them on yir feet and move on from this little hill immediately!"

The tramp bent down and took off his old boots, which were worn and dusty, no laces—a piece of lace tied across the center—and his toes sticking out at the front, holes in the soles. He put them down. Then he stretched out his feet and picked up one boot that the little man had brought. He put it on his foot and it just fit perfectly! Then he picked up the other one, put it on, and it fit perfectly.

And the tramp stood up. When he stood up, the pain of his feet were gone. He wanted to be on his way, he felt so free! His hunger pains were gone, he just wanted to walk on.

But he could not walk away. He bent down, as close as he could above the little man, and said, "Little man, I am thankful fir what you've done for me."

And the little man said, "Does yir feet feel good now?"

He said, "They feel wonderful. They feel wonderful!"

And the little man said, "Cuid you walk now, auld man?"

He said, "Walk! I cuid walk for miles! I'll be on my way and leave ye in peace."

But the little man said, "Stop!"

And the tramp said, "Why?"

"Oh, don't go away right now," said the little man.

The tramp was a wee bit worried because he thought the little man was going to take the boots back from him.

And the little man said, "Before ye go, I want ye tae make me a promise!"

The tramp thought, "Make ye a promise?" "I'll make ye a promise," said the tramp. "What is yir promise?"

The little man said, "Listen very carefully because I'm gaunna tell you something."

And the tramp listened.

The little man said, "Now, you have got some boots."

The tramp said, "Yes, I have got some boots, some beautiful boots like I never had before in my life. I've seen people with boots but not nothing like this! And I've admired people's beautiful boots along the way but I never saw boots like this before in my life. And are they really mine?"

And the little man said, "Yes, they're yours. But make me one promise! These boots will carry you on yir journey for evermore, till the end of yir life. They'll never need to be cleaned, they'll never wear, they'll never be worn out. You'll never have sore feet anymore—providin on one thing . . ."

"And what is that?" said the old tramp.

"That ye never tell a soul where you got them! Will you promise me that?"

The old tramp turned round to the little man and he said, "I make ye my promise . . ."

And the little man held out his hand. The tramp took the little man's hand—just a wee wee hand in his—and he shook hands with the little man.

"Now," said the tramp, "I'll be on my way. Can I go?"

"Well," said the little man, "you can go."

And the old tramp walked on the road, never even looked back, left the little man on the little hill by himself. The tramp went on his way. He felt no pain in his feet and no hunger pains. He just wanted to walk on and on, for ever! He travelled on for miles and miles and he travelled for a year, he travelled for two years . . . And wherever the old tramp went, every night he took off his boots, and placed them beside his head when he went to sleep. And when he woke up in the morning his beautiful boots were there beside him as clean and polished like they had never ever walked a single step! And the tramp loved these boots like he had never loved anything in his life. Although he had walked many many miles, the tramp never felt tired.

So one day the summer came again. He came to this river. And the sun was shining, the day was so beautiful. The old

tramp thought—he wasn't tired and his feet weren't sore—
but he thought his boots were so beautiful, he was ashamed
when he put his dirty feet in them. So he thought he'd walk
down to the river and wash his feet—to fit his beautiful
boots! He walked down to the river, took off his beautiful
boots and placed them by his side.

He was washing his old feet in the river, cleaning his
toenails so's he could put them back into his beautiful boots
and feel no shame . . . when who should come walking up the
river but a fisherman, who was fishing the river from pool to
pool, from pool to pool. He came to the pool where the old
tramp was sitting. And the fisherman was amazed when he
came up and saw the old tramp washing his feet.

But he stopped and said, "Hello, auld man!"

The old tramp looked round. There was the fisherman with
his fishing bag on his back and his fishing rod. He said,
"Hello!"

"Ye're washin yir feet?" said the fisherman.

"Yes," said the tramp, "I'm washin my feet. Because the
day is hot."

And then the fisherman looked: beside the old tramp sitting
was a pair of boots, the most beautiful boots that the fisherman had ever seen in his life! Then he looked at the tramp in
rags, torn coat, long beard, straggly hair—and beside him sat
the most beautiful boots he'd ever seen. "Tell me," said the
fisherman, "are you a tramp?"

"Well," said the old man, "people call me that. I have
walked many many miles—I am a tramp."

"I suppose," said the fisherman, "ye've been many places?"

"Yes," said the old old man, "I've been many places."

"And you've seen many sights?"

"Yes," said the old tramp, "I've seen many sights."

"But tell me truthfully," said the fisherman, "how in the
world could an auld tramp like you own such beautiful boots?"

And the tramp turned round and smiled. "These boots," he
said, "they be mine!"

"But," the fisherman said, "you've after told me you're a tramp!"

"Yes," said the old man, "I'm a tramp."

"But how," said the fisherman, "could a tramp own these boots, so beautiful like that—did you steal them?"

"No," said the tramp, "I never stole them. They're mine!"

"Did you buy them?" said the fisherman.

"No," he said, "I never brought them. These were given tae me as a present."

The fisherman said, "Luik, I've never seen boots like that before. These boots are fit fir a king—never mind a tramp!"

Then the tramp said, "They were made for a king; they were made for a king a long time ago. They were made fir the King o' the Fairies! And the fairies were so kind tae me because I landed on their little hill and they wanted me to move on, they gave me their boots."

The tramp had broken his promise to the fairies!

The fisherman said, "The fairies, and the Fairy King! Ha-ha-ha!" And he picked up his rod and he walked on.

The tramp watched him while he walked up the river. Then the tramp turned round and he looked—his boots were gone . . . mysteriously disappeared. And then it dawned on him, he had broken his promise to the little man. He was so sad! His boots, the most beautiful boots that had carried him so many many miles, were gone. He sat and he sat for a long long time and he knew in his heart there was no solution to his problem. The fairies had gifted him the boots to move from the little hill because they were going to have a fairy party there.

So he had to get up and walk on his way in his bare feet, till some poor crofter or some poor farmer took pity on him and gave him a pair of old boots. But to the end of his days the old tramp never saw his boots again, because he had broken his promise to the little man who had given him the boots of the Fairy King. And that is the end of my story.

I heard this story a long time ago in Furnace when I was about twelve years old. I think I first heard it from a cousin of my father's, an old man called Willie Williamson whose brother stayed in Carradale.

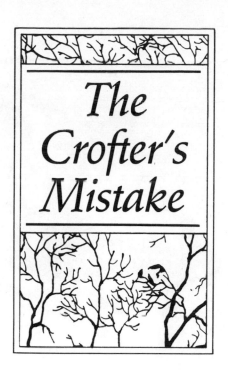

The
Crofter's
Mistake

any many years ago in this island off the West Coast there lived two brothers. Now they had a small croft by the shoreside and naturally they were well off because their mother and father had died many years before and left them plenty of money. The youngest brother's name was Iain, the oldest brother's name was Angus. They had everything they needed—a small croft, a few cattle, and a few sheep and a few goats. But they also had a boat and did a lot of fishing in this island where they stayed.

Now Angus and Iain got on pretty well together after their parents had died. Iain used to go out fishing every morning and evening and he could bring in as much fish as he liked, it only took him a short while. But there was one thing Iain and Angus didn't have in common: Iain loved the seals and used to take fish out of his boat, fling them over the side to feed the seals if he thought he had enough. Now his brother Angus was upset about this.

"Iain, why is it that you feed these animals?" he said. "I hate these things, these seals."

And Iain said, "Well, they hev tae live like you and I, Angus. Luik, we're well off, and we're only taking their food from them. A little bit that we dinna need would feed them."

But Angus was a funny kind of brother, he was a bit morose. Sometimes he got angry and flared into some kind of temper, he was displeased about everything, nothing would

127

content him. The thing he hated most in the world was seals, he hated them for evermore. And when Iain fed them a wee bit, gave them some fish, he said, "Why didn't you bring it here? We could hev used the fish that you've thrown to the seals, and sellt the rest in the village."

"But, Angus, brother," he said, "they have tae live!"

"Och," Angus said, "that's your way, but it's not mine."

But it never came to a quarrel between the two of them. Iain would walk along the beach at night-time and spend all his time sitting on the rocks. The seals would come in around him and he wouldn't pay any attention to them, no way in the world—they were just his friends. But the minute Angus put his foot on the shore there was a splash, and the seals would be gone because he was bad. Anyway, life like that to the two brothers was quite happy, they enjoyed each other's company though they didn't see eye to eye.

One day Iain took four boxes of fish to the market, along to the village where there was a pier. The people in the village were auctioning their fish, putting boxes up for sale. He met this beautiful lassie at the auction, she was standing all alone. She had a book in her hand and a pencil and was looking at all the fish and marking things down, but she wasn't buying anything.

So, after everybody had sold everything they had, and Iain had sold his four boxes of fish, the young woman was still standing there with her book in her hand writing things down. Everybody dispersed, walked away, but she still was standing. So Iain walked up to her. He was a handsome young man, tall, fair hair, blue eyes—the most beautiful man you ever saw.

"Hello!" he said. "Eh, are you buyin or are you sellin?"

"Oh no," she said, "I'm not buyin, I'm not sellin, I'm just having a look to see how much fish is gettin passed, how much is gettin sold and how much fish is comin in."

He said, "Do you work for the government?"

"Oh, oh no, no, I don't work for the government," she

said, "in no way." Young Iain thought that she was a student working for the government or something, in these days taking stock of all the fish that was sold in the island. "No," she said, "I'm just here to see what's going on, and see how much fish is passed through the sale."

So after he had a nice talk to her, he invited her into a wee bar-room for a drink.

"Certainly! I'll go into the bar-room with you." So they went into the fisherman's bar-room and they had a wee drink. It was an ale house—this is many many years ago.

He asked her all the questions in the world about herself but she told him, "I'm an orphan, I've no father and mother. I'm just on my own and I want tae make a record of how much fish is getting sold, how much fish passes through the sale in a year!"

"Oh," Iain said, "that's all right." He didn't worry about it, you see! "Why don't you come out home with me," he said, "tae the croft and we'll have supper together?"

So she went back with him, it wasn't far from the pier, about fifteen minutes' walk to where Iain stayed. When they landed back Angus was sitting at the table. Iain walked in.

Angus said, "And hello, you're back, Iain, you're back."

"Yes," he said, "I'm back. I sold the four boxes of fish and I got a good price for them, but I want you to meet this young woman I met at the saleroom. This young woman's name is Seda, her name is Seda and I met her at the market. She has no relations or no friends. She's callin a check on the fish."

Angus was very morose, a very unpleasant kind of person, you know. Nobody liked him about the village, but everybody liked Iain. Angus was the kind of person you could never get to know. So he said, "And what is the matter with wir fish, is there something wrong, are they not good enough or something?"

"No, no-no," she said, after being introduced to Angus. "No, Angus, that's not the problem at all. I'm just here to keep a check o' all the fish that the people catches and see how much they take out of the sea."

"Well, we don't get enough!" he said. "We could get more if it wasnae for those damn seals who keeps eatin our fish and destroyin our nets!"

And Iain said, "Please, Angus, don't embarrass the woman—start talking about seals again—because ye know they need tae eat as well as us!"

"Och, that's the way you go about it—these *creatures*," he said, "who destroy wir livelihood!"

The young woman never said a word.

But after they had tea together Iain said, "Can I walk ye back to the pier?"

"Oh no, I'm not gaun back to the pier," she said, "I want to go down to the rocks. They tell me that ye've a fine colony o' seals doon by yir croft here on the island."

"Och, we hev hundreds o' seals," he said.

And she said, "Well, what do you think o' them?"

"Oh, they're just my darlings," he said, "I love them to my heart. There's nothing nicer in this world than watching the seals at play; and everything I can spare, though sometimes Angus is upset, I throw anything that I don't need overboard fir them tae have because they hev tae live too, you know."

Angus said, "There you go again, feedin these animals which are no good to anybody. Young woman," he said, "look, I'll tell ye the truth: I hate these things from the word go. They're destroying the things that's wir livelihood."

So Seda said, "Well, they're sea creatures."

"Of course, I know," he said, "they're sea creatures, but why don't they swim along the shore and catch their own fish instead o' robbin wir nets and waitin till we catch fish for them!"

But Seda didn't argue in any way with him.

Iain said, "Come on then, I'll walk ye to the rocks and show you the seals."

"Look, I'll be all right," she said, "I'm sure you can find something else fir yoursel tae do."

So Iain said, "Okay," and the young woman started to walk away. But he had a notion in his head that he loved this young woman. He called after her, "Where can I see ye again?"

She said, "You can find me if you want me!"

"Where will I find you?" he said.

"I'm only here for a short stay, but," she said, "part o' my time'll be spent watchin the seals on the rocks—if you want to find me, you'll find me there."

So he bade her good-bye and she walked away to the rocks.

Angus turned around. "Look, Iain, that's a queer creature! That's a queer kind of woman," he said, "I hope you're no thinkin that mebbe you and she can get together, because her opinions is not the same as mine. She's like you—she loves these creatures that destroys everything that we fought for, destroys wir nets and wir things."

"But, Angus," he said, "the seals are people just like you and me, they need tae live, they need tae eat!"

"Well they're not gaunnae eat out o' wir nets! They're catchin the things that we should catch!"

But Iain didn't want to argue with his brother Angus. So after everything was done Iain started out the door, to walk down to the beach to see his seals once more.

And Angus said, "Where are ye gaun?"

"Ach, I'm going down to the beach," he said, "once more."

"Och, you're going down there again, down again, among yir own kind of folk—you wouldnae stay and talk wi yir brother," he said, "and have a wee dram wi yir brother! Or find something else tae do. You would rather spend yir life doon with the seals—your kind o' folk!"

But Iain didn't want to argue with him. So he walked away down to the seal bay, and on the rocks, sure enough, there sitting was the young woman. She was enjoying herself and all the seals were playing themselves on the rocks—some were sitting basking in the sun, some were lying on their sides, and some were grunting and carrying on, doing all the things that seal people really do. And she really was enjoying it. So he walked down and sat beside her. They talked for a long long time. Iain fell in love with her, and he told her this.

"Look, Seda, I love you more than anything in the world. I'm a lonely man with my brother," he said, "and he's not an easy person tae live wi."

"I have no people in this world," she said, "I'm only here for a short stay."

So he invited her back to the house once more. Naturally, Iain fell more in love with Seda, and as time passed, to cut a long story short, they got married. And Iain brought her back to the house to live with him and his brother Angus. Angus didn't humor her very much, he didn't think very much of her, but Iain loved her from his heart. And they lived very happily. They did their own things: Iain went fishing every day, she helped out on the croft and did everything under the sun that needed to be done. She tried to please Angus to the best of her ability, but there was no way in the world she could. In the evening when they sat down by the fireside, all Angus's talk was about the seals, how much he hated them and how he hated the seal-folk. But Iain and his wife, they really loved each other, and when they got fed up and bored with Angus's talking, the two of them would move off to bed.

But one morning Angus was feeling not too well. Now they set nets for fish, *forbyes*[1] taking care of the croft. And Iain said, "I'll manage myself, Angus, seein you're not feelin too well."

Seda carried up breakfast to Angus in bed, gave him a cup of tea. He wasn't very pleased, he never had a very good word

---

[1] *forbyes*—as well as

for her. And she said to Iain, "Angus is no able tae get up this morning."

"Ach, I'll manage on my own," Iain said.

So Seda kissed him farewell and wished him a good day. Iain took the boat and rowed away to set his nets and do his fishing.

Now Angus, he's lying upstairs in bed. So Seda busied herself around the kitchen, did everything that needed to be done—milked the goats and everything around the croft—the best she could do. She took Angus his dinner, up to him in bed, but he still was bad-tempered, spoke harshly to her. He couldn't even realize that his brother had a young wife and he had nothing! Possibly it was remorse that was bothering him more than anything else.

And every time she came up he was always saying, "I hope he has a good day and I hope the seals disna bother him very much."

But the day passed by and Seda came out—she waited at the doorway. She waited and waited. The day passed but Iain never came back. She went up and told Angus.

"Angus," she said, "Iain's not home yet." Now it was about evening.

"Ach well, he's prob'ly out wi his friends," he said, "round the isle. Whatever you do, don't worry about him—he's prob'ly away feedin his friends in the island, his friends the seals!"

But the night passed by and Iain never came back; and the next day and the next evening, he never came back. And a week passed—he never returned. By this time Angus managed to get down on his feet, he was all right again. And Seda started to tell him about Iain disappearing in the sea.

She said, "Angus, ye'll have to go and notify the police, tell the whole country that Iain is amissing, we've got to get his body back and bury him somewhere."

"Och, he's gone," Angus said, "he's lost in the sea, prob'ly his boat capsized an he's drowned. You'll never see him anymore."

There was a weeping and a wailing, and she cried, she was vexed. And she did everything; Angus never helped her very much. But Iain never returned. Angus bought another boat and she stayed on to keep house for him. Though the two of them couldn't see eye to eye, she did everything under the sun, but they could never exchange a sensible word between them.

Then one evening she told him, "Angus, I'm very sick."

"What's wrong with you! Are you worried about your husband?" he said. "He's gone with his *friends*—at's all ye need tae worry about—he's gone with his friends!"

"Angus," she says, "ye'll have tae go for the doctor."

"Och, why am I to go for the doctor!" He says, "Are ye ill or are ye sick or something?"

She says, "Angus, I'm gaunna have a baby."

"Och dear, oh dear-oh dear-oh me," he says, "you're gaun to have a baby—well, ye'll jist hev tae have a baby!"

It was an old bicycle he had, he cycled to the village and notified the doctor, the doctor came. Sure enough, Seda had a bonnie wee baby—a lassie!

Many weeks had passed since the disappearance of Iain and now there was a bonnie wee baby, a girl had been born. And Angus began to change, he treated them very casually, very nicely.

He said, "What are ye gaunna call her—the baby, the wee baby girl?" It was the first baby he'd ever seen in his life because he didn't have any sisters or brothers, but the one brother who was lost at sea.

"Well," she said, "Angus, I think I'll call her after myself, 'Seda,' after mysel."

So they had reported to the authorities and they'd searched for Iain's body but he never was found, they found the boat but they never got him. "Well, we'll have to make arrange-

ments, you know," he said, "because this croft and the land is
between my brother and me, and now if you want to stay
here with your wee baby daughter, half o' this place, what my
brother Iain owns," he said, "is yours. And I'm sure we'll try
and get along together as best as possible."

Seda was very pleased about this. "There's nothing else I
can do . . . where can I go? I've no place else to go," she said,
"Iain was my husband and you are his brother."

So they stayed in the croft and Angus went on doing the
fishing. Seda took care of the croft and the animals, she
milked the goats, took care of the cow, looked after the croft
the best she could. And naturally wee Seda grew up to be the
bonniest wee lassie in the world. When she started toddling
round the croft, old Angus, the brother who'd be getting a
wee bit old by this time, just loved her like nothing in this
world—there was nothing he loved better than his wee niece!
He cuddled her, kissed her and took her with him every place
he went, took her sailing in the boat, taught her about the
seals, told her how to hate the seals and how the seals had
destroyed her father! But Seda didn't worry about this, she
said, "Okay, that's okay," because she knew her uncle loved
her.

But one night, after young Seda had grown up to be about
six years old, she sat on the chair next to Uncle Angus. She
loved him past the common.

Her mother, Seda, said, "I want to take a walk. I'll see yese
in a wee while." She went for a walk down to the beach.

And Angus said to his niece, "Come tae your Uncle Angus.
Your mammy's gaun for a walk, and I'll tell ye a wee story!"
So he told her a wee story, she fell asleep in his lap and he
carried her up, put her to bed. He waited and he waited, he
waited and waited, but her mother never came back. Her
mother never came back from the beach. She just disappeared
completely.

Next morning young Seda was crying for her mother.
"Your mammy's gone," he said.

He walked down to the village, took Seda with him, reported her mother's disappearance to the police. They searched the shoreside, searched the village, everywhere, but Seda was gone, they couldn't find a trace of her! She was gone for ever. And Angus shook his fist at the shoreside. "It's these people, these seal-folk, they've taken her away, they stole everything that I loved in this world! They take my fish, they took my brother and took my little girl's mother—I'll get revenge on these people in my own time in my own way."

Now Seda was left with her Uncle Angus in this croft on her own. There was nothing else for him to do—she was six years old—he reared her up. Another six years passed and now she was twelve years old. She'd lived with her Uncle Angus all these days in this croft. And he'd sent her to school, walked to meet her and took her back, took care of her—he loved her like nothing else in this world!

But during this period of time Seda, when she had nothing else to do, would spend all her time on the beach sitting on the rocks, swimming out from the shore. The seals were her friends, she spent all her time with them. And Angus began to tell her about these people. "Look, Seda, they took yir mother, they took your father, don't let them take you!"

She says, "Uncle Angus, they never took my father."

"Well, where's their bodies? Where have they gone? Your daddy's disappeared, yir daddy loved these people and yir mammy loved these people, and," he says, "you love them. Seda, luik, don't join these people! Because if ye do, ye'll be gone for ever and they'll never return ye.'"

"But," she says, "Uncle Angus, there's nothing to do with them—they're lovely. I love their life, they're free and they swim in the sea!"

He says, "It's okay, they swim in the sea, and they come and steal my fish in my nets."

"But," she says, "Uncle Angus, they hev tae live too, and

they need something tae eat! They're jist like you and me, jist
lovely creatures."

Seda swam among the seals and she talked to them. The
more she spent her time on the beach, the more Angus got
upset. And he tried to tell her.

But one night he went on a drinking spree and he went
home. When he landed there the house was dark. No tea was
made, nothing. He searched for Seda, tottering about under
the influence of drink. She was gone. He walked down to the
beach, there she was sitting and about fifteen or sixteen seals
were all gathered round her. He rushed down to the shore and
caught her by the arm, he dragged her back to the house.
"Seda, I love you more than anything in this world, but," he
said, "you'll never join these people." So he took her into the
house to where he used to kill the goats. He took a carving
knife—"Now, you'll never be able to tae join these people.
My father," he said, "and my grandmother told me a long
time ago: there's only one way to stop a human fae joinin the
seal people—when you chop off their fingers and you chop off
their toes—I'm gaunna do the same tae you."

"But, Uncle!" she screamed, and she shouted and she cried.
But he held her fast under a drunken stupor and chopped off
the points of her toes, and he chopped off the points of her
fingers.

"Now," he said, "you'll never join these people and go
away fae me!" Then he left her, with parts of her fingers and
parts of her toes chopped off.

She never said a word, she never cried. She lay in her bed
and suffered for two or three days. Angus came up and he
coaxed her to have food, coaxed her to come down after he'd
come to his senses. But no way would she speak to him—no
way in this world, she wouldn't even talk to him! Seda lay in
pain and agony for two weeks, never ate or never spoke for
two weeks.

But finally it came a time when Angus had to go out on the

sea to fish. As much as he loved Seda, he had his duty to perform and go for his fish. So this one day he took his boat and rowed out in the middle of the sea. And he said, "At'll fix her. She'll never join them now because I love her too much. They took my brother, they took his wife, but they'll never take her!"

He rowed out in the boat in the middle of the sea and cast his net. The day was calm and beautiful, the sun was shining. "Now," he said, "I'll have a good fishin today." And he took the oars in his hands, he rowed the boat forward—but all in a moment he was surrounded by about a hundred seals. They came from all parts, they came round the bow of the boat and they came behind the boat and they came by the sides of the boat. They caused such a storm and such a disturbance around the boat, it capsized. The seals—dozens of them, old ones and young ones, big ones and wee ones—capsized the boat and he fell into the water. He tried to swim to the boat and up came the seals, they attacked him, snapped off the points of his fingers and they snapped off the points of his toes. He tried to get away but he was attacked from all angles, every single seal snapped at his fingers and snapped at his toes. They didn't want to do anything else. He swam as best he could, and when he reached the beach he looked at his hands—they were bleeding, his fingers were almost gone and his toes were almost gone. He sprauchled up onto the beach and lay for a long long time. His hands and feet bleeding, he crawled on his hands and knees, he was so exhausted when he reached his own croft—in a terrible state!

"Oh these curséd animals," he said, "they did this tae me, they took my fingers and they took my toes." He looked at his bleeding feet, there was not a whole toe left. He looked at his hands, his fingers were nearly gone, snapped off by the seals! But he survived. They didn't want to kill him, just teach him a lesson. When he landed in the house he called, "Seda, Seda, come and help me! Seda, please help me! I've

lost my fingers, I've lost my toes—please, Seda, help me!"
But the house was empty. There was not a soul there, not a
soul. He searched around, he walked, even though his feet
were bleeding and his hands. He walked around the house,
but Seda was gone.

So for two days he lay in agony and pain with his fingers
and his toes. And he swore to himself, "They did this to me,
they'll never do it to me again. They took my brother, they
took my sister-in-law, and they took my child that I really
loved, even though I did such a terrible thing tae her when I
was drunk. But," he said, "they'll never do this to me again."
And for four more days he lay in agony and pain with his
fingers and his toes.

But after he came to himself and got himself fixed up, he
said, "I'm leavin, never more will I return to this place." So
with his hands bandaged and his feet fixed as best he could, he
closed the door of the cottage. Taking all his belongings that
he ever possessed, that he could carry, he says, "I'm going."
And he shook his fist at the sea, "I'll never return again! You
can have it, Iain, you can have it, Seda; you can have everything I own, but," he says, "never again will you have the
company of me!"

And he walked away, left the croft and everything behind
him. He managed to walk to the village, got attention for his
hands and feet, and he had enough money to keep him for
evermore. He said, "I'm gaun off and find mysel a place in a
glen far away from the sea, far away from the seals, where
people disna know what a seal is." And he went on his way
. . . and he was gone.

About three weeks later, when the cottage on the shoreside
was dark and the sun had set, three seals came swimming
towards the croft. A big bull seal, a female seal, and a half-
grown seal swam towards the beach. They looked at the
cottage and the cottage was dark. One turned to the other and
they nodded, they said, "That is it!" But the funny thing was,

the young, half-grown female seal, half her flippers were gone—half her tail flipper and her front flippers were cut across. They swam into the beach and looked at the dark cottage, the boat was pulled up and the nets were hung up to dry. The three of them came up on the beach and looked all around, then they turned and swam away. They were gone for ever.

The cottage remained waste, the croft remained empty for a very long time, till someone came along and bought it. But they never realized the story behind the croft, what had happened in that cottage. And that is the last of my wee story.

———

People of the present day have little understanding and knowledge of life that existed among the crofting people on the islands many many years ago. Their beliefs and their stories were most important to them. Crofting folk still have the traditional tales that were passed down to them, but they don't like to speak about the stories.

When I left school at fourteen back in Argyll, 1942, there was little to do. So every little job you could get a shilling or a penny for meant the world to you. There was an old man in his seventies, Duncan Bell, he worked in a stone quarry but he loved fishing. He retired the same year I left school, and he was a great fisherman. Old Duncan Bell and I were good friends. So one day he said to me, "Duncan, would ye like to row the boat along tae Minard? We can dig a pail o' worms and I'll give ye a shillin." Now a shilling was a lot of money in these days. I said, "Sure, Duncan!"

So the old man got his small rowing boat and a graip, also a packet of cigarettes. He and I set along the shore; the old man sat in the back smoking Woodbine and I rowed the boat in to Minard. But when we pulled into the beach the tide wasn't full out, there wasn't enough room to dig worms because the sand wasn't showing.

He said to me, "Duncan, it'll be about an hour, maybe an hour and a half, before the tide is fit for hus to dig worms."

Well, it was about the month of October, it was a nice day, too warm for a fire. And the bay below Minard wus famed for seals. We sat on the beach and then the seals came in, not very many, maybe two or three.

I said, "Duncan, tae pass the time away, why don't you tell me a wee story?"

He said, "Duncan, this story came to me many years ago, it was a long time before you were even born. It could hae been my grandmother or my uncle or my great-granduncle who told the story, but it was told to me by my mother. Duncan, as far as I believe, my granny and my great-granny came from the Outer Hebrides. This story could have happened oot in the Western Isles a long time ago; it could hae been Islay, Barra, Jura, Gigha, or ony o' these islands."

It goes to show you, these people enjoyed the company of seal-folk, it's another world, you see! The world of the seal-folk had more appeal to them than the human world. Iain had joined the seal-folk, then his wife had rejoined them, and then Seda—even when her uncle cut off her fingers thinking that she'd have no fins to swim by. But she went, even with half her flippers. When the three of them returned that night and saw the croft all dark, they were happy and pleased.

It's not supposed to be romantic! Every story hasn't got a good ending. You can't say, "They lived happy ever after," it's not that way at all with the seal-folk. It's no fairy tale. These people only revenge an injury. I mean, they could have killed him if they'd wanted to, but they didn't. They took his fingers and took his toes, the same as he had done to one of their family. As far as the seals were concerned, Seda was one of their people. That was an eye for an eye and a tooth for a tooth.

After old Duncan told me this story I said to him, "I would love tae be, tae have the command o' bein one of the seal-

people." And he explained, "In my beliefs in my time ye cannae be one of the seal-people—in on'y one way you can—unless your father or your mother had married one of the seal-folk or made love tae one of them." Duncan didn't mean that the human being makes love to the seal as an animal. The human being makes love to the seal as a person, who is a seal! It's a "seal-woman" or a "seal-man." The seal has the power to take the form of the human. Now these children who are born of a human and a seal have the power to transform into either, be a human or be a seal.

The
Broonie's
Farewell

any years ago there lived a small farmer on a hill farm in the West Highlands of Scotland. He and his wife had this wee farm between them. They were very poor off, they didn't have very much to start with. But as years went by he became a rich man, and when he was middle-aged he had a wee son. The mother and father loved this wee boy dearly. And his mother was such a kindly woman she couldn't see anything going wrong with him; they gave up everything in the world they really needed for the sake of their son. And the son returned it every way possible, he was really good to his mother and father, helped in every way he could. If ever there was a job needing to be done about the place he would always say, "Daddy, I'll do it." His mother would say, "No, son, just dinna hurry yourself, take your time and jist help your daddy whenever possible."

So it came a Saturday afternoon. By this time the laddie was about eleven years old. The old woman was sitting in the kitchen and she said, "Can youse two men no find a job fir yoursels? Because I'm gaun to bake."

And the father said, "Come on," to the laddie, "that's a sign that me and you are no wantit!"

So they walked out of the house and he said, "Daddy, what are we gaunnae do?"

"Well, son, I'll tell you what we're gaunnae do," he said. "We've got everything done, hay's all cut, so we'll need to go in and clean up the barn because it's gettin kind o' tottery. I'm beginnin to fa' ower things in the mornin when I go in there."

145

"All right," said the wee laddie, "I'll go and get a wheelbarra, Daddy, and we'll clean out the barn."

So the wee laddie got a wheelbarrow, *hurled*[1] it into the barn. And the man's picking up old bags and all kinds of stuff, he's putting it in the barrow. But hanging behind the door of the barn inside was a coat and a pair of breeches and a pair of hose. They were covered in cobwebs.

The wee laddie reached up. "Okay, Daddy," he says, "here's some old clothes."

"Oh no, son," he says, "no, don't touch that!"

"Why, Daddy," he says, "it's only old rags."

"No, son," he says, "it's no rags. While your mother's bakin we'll keep oot o' her way . . . and we hevnae much tae dae in here, we're nearly finished . . . sit doon there and I'll tell ye a wee story."

So the farmer took a pitchfork and raked up a bunch of hay, he made a seat. "Now," he said to the wee boy, "sit doon here, son, and I'll tell you aboot that coat, breeches, and the hose . . . Many years ago, long before you were born, when me and yir mother cam here, this place was pretty run doon and we didna have very much money. I got it at a very cheap rent. We cam up here and we workit away hard, both your mother and me, and tried tae make this place intae a kind o' decent fairm. Well, we hadna been here for over a year and things was really tough.

"And one night late, about the month o' October, yir mother and I were sittin doon tae a wee meal, at we didna hae very much at that time, when a knock cam to the door. And your mother said, 'Go and see who that is at this time o' night."

"So naturally I went oot, and there standin at the door was an auld man."

"What kind o' man, Daddy?" the wee boy said. "What kind o' man was he?"

---

[1] *hurled*—wheeled

"Well," he said, "he was just an ordinary auld man, but he wisna very big and he had a white beard. But he had the two bluest eyes that ever I saw in my life. So I asked him what he wanted.

"He said, 'I'm just an auld man and I thought you mebbe have some work, or cuid gie me shelter for the night.'

"So your mother shouted tae me, 'Who is it, John?'

" 'It's an auld man luikin for shelter.'

" 'Well,' she said, 'bring him intae the kitchen!'

"So I said, 'Ye better—'

" 'No, no, no,' he said, 'I can't come intae the kitchen.' The old man wadna come into the kitchen even though yir mother cam to the door. An she coaxed him, but he wadnae come, in any way.

"So wi yir mother being a kind-herted sowl, she asked him, 'Are ye hungry, auld man?'

" 'Oh,' he said, 'I'm hungry, yes, I'm hungry.'

" 'Wad ye like something tae eat?'

" 'Oh, I would love something tae eat. Cuid ye give me a bowl o' porridge an milk?' And naturally, that's what me an yir mother wis haein that night—porridge and milk.

"So yir mother filled a big bowl and I carriet it oot tae him and gied it tae him in his two hands. And I tuik him intae the barn, I said tae him, 'There auld man, ye can find shelter fir the night-time.'

"Well," the farmer said, "I put him in the barn, an," he said, "believe it or not what I'm gaunnae tell ye, that auld man stayed wi me fir six months and I never saw a harder worker in my life. I had practic'ly nothing tae dae round the place. He was up, first thing in the mornin he startit tae work, tae the last thing at night he was still workin. He had everything about this place prosperin like it never prospered before. I never lost an animal of any kind, I had the greatest crops that ever I cuid ask for and I cam in an offered him wages, but he wouldnae have any. Or he wouldnae come intae the house, all he wanted tae do was sleep in the barn.

"Well after workin fir about six months yir mother took pity on him. And one night she sat down special hersel and made him a coat because he was ragged, and she made him a pair o' breeches cut doon fae mine and she knittit him a pair o' hose. And one mornin when she cam oot wi his bowl o' porridge, she brought them and placed them beside his bowl. Later in the mornin when I cam oot, the coat, the breeches, and the hose wis gone, an the bowl was empty—his auld breeches and his coat wis hung behind the door. And there they've been hung, son, fir over eleven year. And *remember*: someday this farm will pass on tae you but promise me, as long as you own this place ye'll never part with these breeches, or that coat or thae hose!"

"No, Daddy," he said, "I never will."

And when the man passed on and the young laddie got the farm, the breeches and the coat and the hose hung behind the door till it passed on to his son, and that's the last of my wee story.

————

People were very privileged to be visited by the Broonie. And if he ever visited any place at any particular time, his visit was never forgotten. Word of it always passed down, from generation to generation, and this is where "The Broonie's Farewell" really came from. An old traveller man told me this story a long time ago when I was very young. He said it really happened, he was suppposed to have been at the farm— away back in the highlands of Argyllshire, near Rannoch Moor, I don't know the name of the farmer in the story, but the Broonie didn't care for anybody without a "Mac" in their name. The Broonie was the patron spirit of the MacDonalds.

The breeches the Broonie left in the barn were short, just came below the knee, the hose was pulled up to meet them. They laced down the side of the leg and were made of corduroy. They hung at the back of that door for years and years, and were never allowed to pass away from that place.

*You're not to pay the Broonie, you see. You can thank him,
but the minute you pay him, you're finished. He wouldn't
take any money, and when she'd left the clothes down beside
his bowl, he thought, "That's your payment—we've nae
mair use for you" . . . he was gone! So that's why the old
man told the laddie to hang on to the coat, he thought maybe
the Broonie might come back.*

GLOSSARY

Duncan Williamson's dialect is rich and flexible: it varies according to who is listening as well as to the content of a particular story. With a command of both English and Scots, he swings in either direction, towards a dominantly English element on one occasion and a fuller degree of Mid-Scots on another. Part of the idiom of the Highland tales can be traced to Duncan's home area, where he heard the stories. He grew up on Loch Fyneside in a community of people who spoke Highland English, an inflected English with a few Scots words and some Gaelic words and phrases. Duncan does not distinctly remember speaking "English" with the old crofters, fishermen, quarry workers, and builders who were his informants; he prefers to think of their common language as "Highland Scots." He acquired Lowland Scots after he left home at fifteen:

> . . . Because the thing was, I had to go out in this world among all these strangers, and sit round the campfires, which was very popular in these days. And I know that sometimes I was a wee bit backward, I was very Highland talking. My own brother was ashamed of me because I had such a Highland tongue. Naturally, after about eighteen months you get accustomed . . . you've got to be able to change. My language has changed after twenty-five years . . .

How much dialect to use in publication is a moot point. If the book is to reach an international audience, then a viable

151

combination of conventional usage and original speech has to be created. I have presented the stories in a language that is neither strict Scots nor wholly standard English. The narrator's dialect has been transcribed directly in the dialogues within the stories, and the balance of the narrative has been anglicized for effective communication in print. A few words, idiomatic phrases, and cant in the stories have been defined in footnotes; meanings of other Scots words are shown below. All definitions are Duncan's and may or may not conform to dictionary entries.

A

ae—one
all fared well—nothing else happened
an—although, if
away a long way—from a long way off

B

barrikit—a large bow-shaped tent
ben—further in
bing—a large number, crowd
bletherin stories—foolish tales and cracks
bonnie—beautiful, pretty, fine

C

ceilidh—party
clift—cliff
clinker-built—made of interlocked strips of wood, typically Norwegian
cool—cowl, hood
country folk—non-travellers
country hantle—non-travellers
crack—to discuss news and gossip; tell stories
cratur—dear creature (often used affectionately)
croft—small farm
crusie—small open lamp with a pith of cotton burned with paraffin

D

day; the day—today
diddler—someone who sings dance tunes with nonsense syllables
dinnae—don't
doubt—suspect

F

fae—from
fearin—entire
fit—foot; ready
forebyes—as well as

G

gadgie—man
garron—highland pony
gentle kind o' cratur—kindly soul
girnin—fretting peevishly
graip—iron-pronged fork used for farm work
grannies' cracks—old wives' tales
greet—cry
greetin and roarin—crying and shouting
gurie—girl

H

hantle—people
happed—covered
heck—a wooden press for holding hay so a cow can stand and chew

het—warmed (up), comfortable
hurled—wheeled

I

it took me . . . busy—she was just enough for me (to carry)

K

kippered—salted and dried in smoke
knowe—hillock
kye—cows

L

learn—to teach
lane—self
lea—to leave

M

morn—tomorrow

N

newsin—telling news
night—tonight

O

oxter—the underarm, (at the) bosom; to help up by the armpits; *in her oxter*—under her arm; *my oxters*—both arms

P

pick—a small amount
piece—sandwich
puckle—small quantity

R

ron—seal (Gaelic)

S

saltie—a sailor, fond of the water

Shanness . . . hantle's wee pinchen—Shame on you . . . that's a child belonging to country folk
shune—shoes
sic—such
skelped—slapped
sowl—person; animal
sprauchled—clambered
sweerin—reluctant
swinge—to whine; an ill-tempered child

T

thae—those
the're—there is
tottery—messy

W

wag-at-the-wa clock—pendulum wall clock
was cowped—had fallen over
waste—empty
wean—child (*wee one*)
wee puckle—small amount
wee puckle hay the day—small amount of hay today
well on—under the influence of alcohol
what's about—what though, what would happen
wheesht—quiet, hush!
whinge—cried and whined
wir—our
woein—being sad, lamenting

Y

youse—you (plural)